"*The Christian Leader's Worldview* is a helpful resource for anyone desiring to understand and embrace a biblical approach to leading and living. Throughout the thoughtful discussion and heartwarming poetry, author Michael LaPierre offers very practical insights for developing a Christian worldview and encourages the reader to passionately lead with that foundation. Anyone leading a business, organization, church, or home will be helped and challenged by this easily-read volume. The book provides significant help for staff development and small-group discussion."

—**Dr. Ron Allen**, Pastor, Bible Baptist Church

"Michael LaPierre's book, *The Christian Leader's Worldview*, is a must-read for every Christian who is in a leadership position at work, home, school, or church. Michael's principles of leadership are insightful and useful for self-analysis, as well as, teaching others about what it means to be a Christian leader. Michael's use of Scripture, knowledge from other Christian authors, and contemporary examples helps the reader to understand the source of, and application of, his principles."

—**Bruce E. Winston**, PhD,
Professor of Business and Leadership
Regent University

"As an anthology of sorts, *The Christian Leader's Worldview* addresses many of the contemporary issues we face individually as Christians and corporately as the Church. By pairing Scripture with insights that are both practical and proven, the author provides a perspective on leadership that is intently focused on honoring God and having a greater impact on the world around us. Read the book and you'll have a greater appreciation for the wisdom of Scripture and its application to your daily life."

—**Bruce Snyder**, Principal & Senior Consultant,
The Westover Group

"Mike LaPierre has clearly captured the depth and breadth of what it means to be a Christian leader. The personal testimonies and humorous anecdotes make this a must-read for leaders in the 21st century. This book is a spot-on framework for leadership and successful living. I can't wait to share this with my friends, family, and colleagues."

—**Gail DePriest,** Director of Executive Leadership & Corporate Relations Clemson MBA

"Does the world really need another book on leadership? Michael LaPierre's exhaustive, scholarly, yet practical work tips the scales to a compelling *yes*! *The Christian Leader's Worldview* is a comprehensive and admirable account of Biblical leadership with a fresh perspective. This book will serve as a definitive study of leadership for years to come. This work offers a portrait of Christian leadership with profound relevance for our troubled times."

—**Gregory Blake,** Chief Engagement Officer, PepWorks International

"Whether leading a small staff or being an executive at a high level, I love Mike's approach to coaching. *The Christian Leader's Worldview* illustrates practical servant leadership and Christian principles that will make me a better leader and be able to guide my team forward."

—**Rick Slagle**
VP of Procurement, Marketing, and Business Development
WYNIT

"My co-worker, Mike LaPierre, certainly understands the value of faith, ethics, unselfishness, and spiritual consciousness in an organizational setting. He lived those same principles throughout all my interactions with him. Everyone should be able to identify, meditate on, internalize, and act on one or more of the leadership principles contained in this great read!"

—**Myron Williams,** Sales President

"It has been my opportunity and pleasure to meet with Mike LaPierre and become acquainted with him. His unwavering commitment to sharing the gospel message with the business community is palpable. Furthermore, there has likely never been a time in the history of America in which a Christian worldview needs to pervade every aspect of the believer's life more. Mike's book will articulate and transfer both of these key learning issues to the reader."

—**Rand Clark**, MBA
Christian Businessman, Church Planter, and Teacher

"Mike LaPierre does an excellent job of taking the many leadership principles found in the Bible and applying them to leadership at all levels and in all walks of life. Mike's passion for developing leaders through a Christian worldview is evident as he builds on the Scriptural foundation to give practical advice to any current and rising leaders. I encourage any leader who is serious about practicing a Biblical approach to read this book and to apply the principles found in it."

—**Dr. Ryan Meers**, Church Planter and Leadership Coach

"Mike LaPierre has shared from the course of his life experiences how to lead, be it organizations, churches, families, or children. The leadership perspectives Mike shares are solidly grounded in the Word of God. Reading this book makes one realize the gift from God to us – the Bible where it is all written. It was very encouraging to me as I read through the chapters while on a train in Italy from Rome to Ancona and back. I highly recommend taking time to read and pray to God to lead as one does."

—**G. Kumar Venayagamoorthy**, PhD

THE CHRISTIAN LEADER'S WORLDVIEW

A Framework for Successful Leadership and Living

MICHAEL J. LAPIERRE

HIGH BRIDGE BOOKS
HOUSTON

The Christian Leader's Worldview
by Michael J. LaPierre

Copyright © 2016 by Michael J. LaPierre
All rights reserved.

Printed in the United States of America
ISBN (Paperback): 978-1-940024-66-0
ISBN (Hardcover): 978-1-940024-72-1
ISBN (eBook): 978-1-940024-67-7

All rights reserved. Except in the case of brief quotations embodied in critical articles and reviews, no portion of this book may be reproduced, stored in a retrieval system, or transmitted in any form or by any means—electronic, mechanical, photocopy, recording, scanning, or other—without the prior written permission from the author.

High Bridge Books titles may be purchased in bulk for educational, business, fundraising, or sales promotional use. For information please contact High Bridge Books via www.HighBridgeBooks.com/contact.

Published in Houston, Texas by High Bridge Books

Unless otherwise indicated, all Scripture quotations are taken from the *King James Study Bible* (previously published as *The Liberty Annotated Study Bible* and as *The Annotated Study Bible*, King James Version). Copyright 1988 by Liberty University.

About the Author

Michael J. LaPierre is a Brown University graduate with Bachelor of Arts degrees in both Organizational Behavior & Management and Political Science. He currently is finishing his Master of Business Administration degree at Clemson University with a focus on Entrepreneurship & Innovation. He is an author, motivational speaker, guest lecturer, and founder and current President of Christian Leadership Worldview International, LLC (clwi.org).

A former professional baseball player, his executive experiences over the past 30 years include VP of Sales, Director of Sales & Marketing, global strategist, entrepreneur, church servant/deacon, and community leader. His diverse executive background and nonprofit experiences have allowed him to gain a comprehensive understanding of the principles of leadership development. Those broad experiences include leadership positions on management teams in companies such as UPS, Arnold Industries, Lily Transportation, and Roadway Express.

With nonprofit, for-profit, ministerial, and athletic experiences as a backdrop, Michael has the proven ability to capture the essence and fundamentals of leadership training and development. He then relates those varied experiences in a communication style that is motivational, powerful, and relevant to today's employees, students, and organizational leaders.

Mike and his wife, Calie, have been married for more than 31 years. They have three adult children: Ryan, Kyle, and Lauren. They also have been blessed with four grandchildren: Emma, Julia, Cooper, and Tanner. Mike and Calie reside in Pickens, South Carolina.

To contact Mike about the possibility of speaking at your next leadership event and/or conducting a leadership conference/seminar, you can reach him via the following:

- mikelapi@gmail.com
- mike@clwi.org
- www.clwi.org

To my wife, Calie…
For loving me in the best and worst of times

To my children—Ryan, Kyle, and Lauren Rose…
For allowing me to become the leader that I needed to be

To my grandchildren…
The future is yours… make a difference

To all my previous and current pastors…
I can't thank you enough

Christian Leadership Defined:

"*The thoughts, desires, passions, and actions of Christian men and women, by the leading of the Holy Spirit and under God's control, for selfless ends.*"

— Michael J. LaPierre

Contents

Preface & Author's Passion _____ XVII

Part 1: The Purpose of Leadership _____ 1
1: The Glory Due His Name _____ 3
2: Proclaiming a Savior _____ 9
3: Making Decisions that Matter _____ 16
4: Embracing God's Word _____ 20
5: A Living Sacrifice _____ 23
6: Developing Others through Coaching _____ 30
7: Surround Yourself with Christian Heroes _____ 36
8: Obedience to God's Call _____ 40
9: Be Silent Before Him _____ 44
10: Sufficiency in Christ _____ 46

Part 2: The Fundamentals of Oranizational Leadership _ 51
11: Project Management 101 _____ 53
12: The Quigley & The Disciplined Leader _____ 71
13: The Power of Team _____ 75
14: The Servant Leader _____ 86
15: Organizational Decision-Making _____ 92
16: Filtering Organizational Noise _____ 96
17: Developing Policy: A Homeschool Primer _____ 98
18: What is Your Communication Strategy? _____ 104

19: Roaring Thunder _____ 111
20: Church Strategy in the 21st Century _____ 114

Part 3: Being Led as a Leader _____ 123
21: Prayer's Guiding Inspiration_____ 125
22: A Spirit-Filled Imagination _____ 128
23: The Whole Counsel of God _____ 130
24: Moved With Compassion _____ 133
25: Remember the Mountains _____ 137
26: Desiring Obedience _____ 140
27: Trust in Me _____ 143
28: Failing to Annihilate _____ 145
29: A Spirit-Filled Church _____ 149
30: Discerning Sin's Allure _____ 151
31: Desperate Need _____ 153
32: In His Presence_____ 155

Part 4: A Leader Sees God in Everyday Living _____ 157
33: The Two-Sided Fence _____ 159
34: This Old House _____ 162
35: Handfuls of Purpose _____ 165
36: God's Lightning Strikes _____ 167
37: Those Pesky Little Fellas _____ 170
38: Those Storm Clouds Yonder _____ 173
39: The Joy of Life _____ 177

PART 5: LEADING AS A PARENT	179
40: A Parent's Roadmap	181
41: Loving Your Children through Letters	185
42: Children Beware	188
43: Where is Your Child's Anchor?	191
44: The Content Family	195
45: Expressions of Love	197
46: Babes in Christ Jesus	199
PART 6: LEADERS ARE CONCERNED FOR THEIR COUNTRYMEN	201
47: The Whitewash Impact	203
48: Casual Trends in Worship	208
49: Have You Noticed?	211
50: The "Me" Generation	213
51: The Cycle of Sin	215
52: The World is Outraged! Why?	218
53: The Adamic Sin Nature of Man	220
54: America's Tipping Point	223
CONCLUSION: IT'S TIME TO STEP UP	229
About Us	231
Endnotes	233

Preface & Author's Passion

While the topic of developing and living out a biblical worldview has been written about by scores of religious scholars and theologians, this book offers a compelling and unique perspective from someone who is just like you. *The Christian Leader's Worldview* is a practical application guide that has been written to challenge the hearts, minds, and souls of individuals living in today's popular culture.

The chapters in this book contain narratives and perspectives that stem from the Bible. The topics discussed are varied purposefully in their content to articulate what it means to have a *Christian leadership worldview*. Everything—from athletics, organizational behavior, performance, materialism, culture, and even issues related to homeschooling—is debated and discussed.

We are in desperate times here in the United States of America, and desperate times call for leaders who will step up and make a difference. Christian leaders need to become more self-aware, confidently and logically defending their positions and points of view while developing a leadership mindset that is different from the rest of the world. Ultimately, leaders must learn to assimilate facts, context, and their environment quickly and decisively to be able to render opinions while holding to traditional values and biblical mindsets.

Although complacency abounds in our country, we must come together as a nation to change the course of history. Leaders should be disciplined enough and have the moral courage to think and act in ways that represent Christian distinctiveness. It is truly a spiritual battle and one that encompasses every decision we make here on God's created earth.

The challenge for each of us is to thoughtfully and prayerfully formulate opinions on the myriad of issues and topics that pass our way each day and then stand up and shout those opinions from the rooftops. Stepping out and having a *Christian leadership worldview* is an act of courage and boldness. We need to not be silenced. We need to stand and fight for our voices to be heard. The bottom line is that we should desire to make a difference for future generations.

Part 1
The Purpose of Leadership

1
THE GLORY DUE HIS NAME

*"And the priests waited on their offices: the Levites also with instruments of music of the Lord, which David the king had made to praise the Lord, because his mercy endureth for ever, when David praised by their ministry; and the priests sounded trumpets before them, **and all Israel stood.**"*
2 Chronicles 7:6

When I read this fascinating account of when the glory of the Lord filled the temple and how the people of Israel reacted in this moment, it gave me chills. What an awesome point in time in our Judeo-Christian heritage. Can you imagine with me just for a second about having the Shekinah glory and radiance of the Lord before your very eyes? It is enough for me to want to stand up and shout, "Hallelujah and praise be to God!"

What is even more exciting and insightful are the circumstances that preceded this miraculous and supernatural event. Can you guess? Yes, it was a time of prayer and dedication unto the Lord!

This particular setting was especially significant in that it was the culmination of one of the most prosperous spiritual periods in the history of the nation of Israel. In a sense, they had it all. They had the right king, the right spirit, the right motivation, and the right praise and adoration along with an intense desire and unity to serve the Lord.

THE RIGHT KING

King Solomon was a humble servant determined to judge aptly this peculiar (separate) people, Israel. God's choice of using King Solomon to build the temple was especially evident and poignant when God visited him and offered a commendation.

> "And Solomon said unto God, Thou hast showed great mercy unto David my father, and hast made me to reign in his stead. Now, O Lord God, let thy promise unto David my father be established: for thou hast made me king over a people like the dust of the earth in multitude. Give me now wisdom and knowledge, that I may go out and come in before this people: for who can judge this thy people, that is so great? And God said to Solomon, Because this was in thine heart, and thou hast not asked riches, wealth, or honor, nor the life of thine enemies, neither yet hast asked long life; but hast asked wisdom and knowledge for thyself, that thou mayest judge my people, over whom I have made thee king: Wisdom and knowledge is granted unto thee; and I will give thee riches, and wealth, and honor, such as none of the kings have had that have been before thee, neither shall there any after thee have the like."
> (2 Chronicles 1:8-12)

Well, there it is. Solomon was only concerned with serving the people and wanted the wisdom and knowledge to be able to do so. He was selfless in the face of his imminent kingship, dominion, and authority over all the land.

The Right Spirit

God's people showed a willingness to do what was right. They wanted the moment to be shrouded in praise, adoration, generosity, and a willing sacrifice unto their Lord.

> "And all the elders of Israel came; and the Levites took up the ark. And they brought up the ark, and the tabernacle, these did the priests and the Levites

> bring up. Also King Solomon, and all the congregation of Israel that were assembled unto him before the ark, sacrificed sheep and oxen, which could not be told nor numbered for multitude."
> (2 Chronicles 5:4-6)

His people were in such a state of worship that the animals that were being sacrificed on the altar could not be numbered. I guess you could say that it was untold and unimagined spiritual sacrifice and generosity.

THE RIGHT MOTIVATION

The motivation of both Solomon and the congregation of Israel is evident as the dedication service unfolds. Scripture reveals that discussions of humility, prayer, supplication, confession, forgiveness, fear, righteous judgment, and blessings were all part of this holy and solemn event. The following verses capture a hint of the true spirit of the occasion.

> "And he stood before the altar of the Lord in the presence of all the congregation of Israel, and spread forth his hands: For Solomon had made a brazen scaffold, of five cubits long, and five cubits broad, and three cubits high, and had set it in the midst of the court: and upon it he stood, and kneeled down upon his knees before all the congregation of Israel, and spread forth his hands toward heaven, And said, O Lord God of Israel, there is no God like thee in the heaven, nor in the earth; which keepest covenant, and showest mercy unto thy servants, that walk before thee with all their hearts: Thou which hast kept with thy servant David my father that which thou hast promised him; and spakest with thy

mouth, and hast fulfilled it with thine hand, as it is this day." (2 Chronicles 6:12-14)

"Hearken therefore unto the supplication of thy servant, and of thy people Israel, which they shall make toward this place: hear thou from thy dwelling place, even from heaven; and when thou hearest, forgive." (2 Chronicles 6:21)

There kneeled King Solomon on a scaffold with his outstretched hands toward heaven above. Oh, if the human mind could only wrap itself around such a deep, moving, and spiritually significant event.

The Right Praise

It makes one wonder if the choir that we read about in 2 Chronicles (see below) will be heard again one day when we get to heaven. What an awe-inspiring and majestic description of what God's people are capable of when they unite in praise and thanksgiving.

"It came to pass, as the trumpeters and singers were as one, to make one sound to be heard in praising and thanking the Lord; and when they lifted up their voice with the trumpets and cymbals and instruments of music, and praised the Lord, saying, For he is good; for his mercy endureth for ever: that then the house was filled with a cloud, even the house of the Lord; So that the priests could not stand to minister by reason of the cloud: for the glory of the Lord had filled the house of God."
(2 Chronicles 5:13-14)

Are you starting to understand the significance of the event? Can you envision the beauty of the moment? An angelic symphony so powerful and so full of the joy of the Lord that you feel like you are being transported before the Lord Himself. Well, we simply will have to wait for that one.

THE RIGHT UNITY

There is no question that the nation of Israel was in one accord in this period of their history. There was so much unity in the Spirit of God that Solomon even mentioned the strangers that were in the land during his dedication prayer. The hearts of the people were melted toward the strangers during this time period.

> "Moreover concerning the stranger, which is not of thy people Israel, but is come from a far country for thy great name's sake, and thy mighty hand, and thy stretched out arm; if they come and pray in this house; Then hear thou from the heavens, even from thy dwelling place, and do according to all that the stranger calleth thee for; that all people of the earth may know thy name, and fear thee, as doth thy people Israel, and may know that this house which I have built is called by my name."
> (2 Chronicles 6:32-33)

So it appears that, when "all Israel stood", God was working in that nation in a special and meaningful way. Both Jew and stranger alike who were willing to submit themselves to a righteous God were included in the holy proclamation from King Solomon.

So let us now try to apply this to today's Christians. What would make you stand in reverence and in awe before our Maker? What conditions would have to be present this side of heaven to motivate you to desire the right king (King Jesus), the right spirit, the right motivation, and the right praise along with an intense desire and unity to serve the Lord? Fortunately, our Creator has provided these conditions for us here on this earth.

> "For in this we groan, earnestly desiring to be clothed upon with our house which is from heaven."
> (2 Corinthians 5:2)

CHRISTIAN LEADERSHIP WORLDVIEW – PRINCIPLE #1

Each time God's people meet for worship or fellowship, we have the privilege to "stand" before our God and give praise and adoration to His name. We have the privilege to choose unity with the brethren, to choose to put on the mind of Christ with the right spirit and motivation, to choose to praise our Savior with an intense desire to see His face, and to choose to rightly divide the Word of God. Joy unspeakable and full of glory!

2
Proclaiming a Savior

> *"Courage is what it takes to stand up and speak;*
> *courage is also what it takes to sit down and listen."*
> ***Winston Churchill***

What a glorious responsibility we have to proclaim the gospel message of Jesus Christ, our Lord and Savior! The Bible so meticulously defines all of the reasoning and the elements of that sacred responsibility. In His Word, God gives us the *who, what, when, where, how,* and *why* of spreading this life-changing, gospel message. He's very descriptive, leaving nothing to the imagination when it comes to evangelism. In addition, God gives us—weak and frail human beings—all of the context we need to understand its impact. Yes, the mighty God of this universe took the time to break down His expectations with childlike simplicity.

In this chapter, we will explore what it means to proclaim the name of Jesus Christ and evangelize the world.

Where?

The scope of the Great Commission is broad. It is not limited by nationality, geographic constraints, or racial boundaries. The Bible tells us to "teach all nations." It is this vision that sets the tone for the enormity of the task at hand. We are to evangelize the entire world.

Who?

The Great Commission is based on the power of our risen Savior. We are called to "go ye therefore." It is a clear directive with authority that Christians (the Church) have a responsibility to proclaim the name of Christ. The world is our mission field, and we must go to teach and to baptize "in the name of the Father, and of the Son, and of the Holy Ghost."

> "Go ye therefore, and teach all nations, baptizing them in the name of the Father, and of the Son, and of the Holy Ghost: Teaching them to observe all things whatsoever I have commanded you: and, lo, I am with you always, even unto the end of the world." (Matthew 28:19-20)

What?

We are obligated to teach, preach, witness, testify, proclaim, and glorify the name of Jesus Christ, our Lord. We have a Christian duty to "shout it out" in the name of our Savior. We are to "ring out" skillfully and passionately a salvation message that will have lasting and eternal consequences. It is a message that can't be dismissed or denied without pricking our spiritual consciences. It forces us to consider and weigh the standards of what ultimate truth looks like. This is the only message the world has ever known that must be reckoned with in absolute terms. Oh, that God would give us that "door of utterance" to proclaim His holy name!

> "So shall my word be that goeth forth out of my mouth: it shall not return unto me void, but it shall accomplish that which I please, and it shall prosper in the thing whereto I sent it." (Isaiah 55:11)

> "And daily in the temple, and in every house, they ceased not to teach and preach Jesus Christ." (Acts 5:42)

> "And when they had appointed him a day, there came many to him into his lodging; to whom he expounded and testified the kingdom of God, persuading them concerning Jesus, both out of the law of Moses, and out of the prophets, from morning till evening." (Acts 28:23)

> "For WHOSOEVER SHALL CALL UPON THE NAME OF THE LORD SHALL BE SAVED. How then shall they call on him in whom they have not believed? And how shall they believe in him of whom they have not heard? And how shall they hear without a preacher? And how shall they preach, except they be sent? As it is written, HOW BEAUTIFUL ARE THE FEET OF THEM THAT PREACH THE GOSPEL OF PEACE, AND BRING GLAD TIDINGS OF GOOD THINGS!" (Romans 10:13-15)

> "So then faith cometh by hearing, and hearing by the word of God." (Romans 10:17)

How?

God wants us to approach the Great Commission in a spirit of boldness. The Word of God provides many verses about how we are to conduct ourselves in this regard. We must not faint. We are to run the race that is set before us diligently.

> "The wicked flee when no man pursueth: but the righteous are bold as a lion." (Proverbs 28:1)

> "And when they had prayed, the place was shaken where they were assembled together; and they were filled with the Holy Ghost, and they spake the word of God with boldness." (Acts 4:31)

> "According to the eternal purpose which he purposed in Christ Jesus our Lord: In whom we have boldness and access with confidence by the faith of him." (Ephesians 3:11-12)

When Christ walked the face of this earth, He disrupted conventional wisdom and proclaimed that He was the Messiah. This was a position that was not very popular with the ruling elite or the citizenry. Quite frankly, many thought he was a madman. Nonetheless, He continued with the proclamation that He was "the way the truth and the life" without fear of retribution, contempt, or death. He was and still is God Almighty.

> "And when he was come into his own country, he taught them in their synagogue, insomuch that they were astonished, and said, Whence hath this man this wisdom, and these mighty works?"
> (Matthew 13:54)

> "Jesus saith unto him, I am the way, the truth, and the life: no man cometh unto the Father, but by me."
> (John 14:6)

The Apostle Paul was also a man of great boldness in the faith. He too risked his life for the furtherance of the gospel. Paul boldly proclaimed his faith everywhere he went. Witnessing became the essence of who he was as a Christian solder.

> "And for me, that utterance may be given unto me, that I may open my mouth boldly, to make known the mystery of the gospel, For which I am an ambassador in bonds: that therein I may speak boldly, as I ought to speak." (Ephesians 6:19-20)

> "And he went into the synagogue, and spake boldly for the space of three months, disputing and persuading the things concerning the kingdom of God." (Acts 19:8)

> "Withal praying also for us, that God would open unto us a door of utterance to speak the mystery of Christ, for which I am also in bonds: That I may make it manifest, as I ought to speak."
> (Colossians 4:3-4)

WHEN?

There is an immediacy to the call of spreading the good news of Christ. Christians must not wait or put on hold what we are expected to do. We live in perilous and apostate times. We must be about the Father's business to bring light to a dying and perverse world. Once again, we can look to the Word of God for our answers when it comes to the urgency of the times.

> "This know also, that in the last days perilous times shall come." (2 Timothy 3:1)

> "Redeeming the time, because the days are evil." (Ephesians 5:16)

> "And that, knowing the time, that now it is high time to awake out of sleep: for now is our salvation nearer than when we believed." (Romans 13:11)

> "Repent: for the kingdom of heaven is at hand." (Matthew 4:18)

> "Say not ye, There are yet four months, and then cometh harvest? Behold, I say unto you, Lift up your eyes, and look on the fields; for they are white already to harvest." (John 4:35)

Why?

Why must we take an assertive position when it comes to witnessing and spreading the gospel message? Are the motivations ideological, philosophical, political, or just a self-centered need to persuade others to our point of view? Is the bottom line our need to be right, and is it all about us? Or, do we selflessly proclaim the salvation message as instruments of God's love and His righteousness to see people come to an eternal and saving knowledge of Jesus Christ? Are we *consumed* with sowing the seeds to point others to heaven's glory and to prevent them from spending an eternity in hell?

> "For the wages of sin is death; but the gift of God is eternal life through Jesus Christ our Lord." (Romans 6:23)

> "In my Father's house are many mansions: if it were not so, I would have told you. I go to prepare a place for you." (John 14:2)

> "And after these things I heard a great voice of much people in heaven, saying, Alleluia; Salvation, and

glory, and honor, and power, unto the Lord our God." (Revelation 19:1)

Christian, are you shouting out the good news of the gospel? Have you made the decision to serve Christ in your life with all of your heart, mind, and soul?

Praise God in the highest!

CHRISTIAN LEADERSHIP WORLDVIEW – PRINCIPLE #2

We need to be ready, willing, and able to heed the call of God to boldly preach the gospel message to the outermost parts of the world. The Great Commission should be the driving force and motivation for Christian servants to be about their Father's work.

3
MAKING DECISIONS THAT MATTER

"If your actions inspire others to dream more, learn more,
do more and become more, you are a leader."
John Quincy Adams

If... then. These are two of the most powerful words in all of the English language. On these two words hang the plight and spiritual destiny of all the human race. We can clearly observe a conditional element in the relationship between each word at the beginning of this chapter along with an incremental and collaborative dynamic and understanding. These two words set the stage for how you will live out your existence here on this earth. God's Word supernaturally captures their impact on mankind. The word, *if*, is used more than 1,500 times in the Bible. How fortunate are we as Christians to have these numerous teaching moments... to have these spiritual cause-and-effect descriptive illustrations to guide us as we formulate a *Christian leadership worldview?*

These words are conditional in that there is a presupposition of an action that must take place prior to an eventual outcome. In other words, there is an inherent understanding in the relationship that some type of thought, event, movement, or directive must commence and take place before an end result occurs. For example, God used the nation of Israel to play out various conditional outcomes as an illustration for King Solomon. He first portrayed the positive conditional ties between Israel's actions (the "if") and what would happen as a result of their actions (the "then").

> "If my people, which are called by my name, shall
> humble themselves, and pray, and seek my face, and

turn from their wicked ways; then will I hear from heaven, and will forgive their sin, and will heal their land." (2 Chronicles 7:14)

All God wanted from the nation of Israel was their commitment and obedience to live righteous and holy lives while making Him their sole spiritual priority. God wanted their complete submission to His authority in their lives.

God went on to personalize His message for King Solomon based on the king's own level of faith, obedience, and commitment.

> "And as for thee, if thou wilt walk before me, as David thy father walked, and do according to all that I have commanded thee, and shalt observe my statutes and my judgments; Then will I establish the throne of thy kingdom, according as I have covenanted with David thy father, saying, There shall not fail thee a man to be ruler in Israel."
> (2 Chronicles 7:17-18)

Then, God took it one step further and gave a clear warning of what the consequences would be for their disobedience in yet another if-then illustration.

> "But if ye turn away, and forsake my statutes and my commandments, which I have set before you, and shall go and serve other gods, and worship them; Then will I pluck them up by the roots out of my land which I have given them; and this house, which I have sanctified for my name, will I cast out of my sight, and will make it to be a proverb and a byword among all nations. And this house, which is high, shall be an astonishment to everyone that passeth by it; so that he shall say, Why hath the Lord done thus

> unto this land, and unto this house? And it shall be answered, Because they forsook the Lord God of their fathers, which brought them forth out of the land of Egypt, and laid hold on other gods, and worshipped them, and served them: therefore hath he brought all this evil upon them."
> (2 Chronicles 7:19-22)

The incremental aspect of the if-then relationship can be seen as we live out our experiences of life either as a nation or individually under God. Generally speaking, the cause-and-effect process of our actions takes much time to mature and to simmer. It is like a great big vat of Italian sauce sitting on the open stove, marinating to perfection… or, perhaps, marinating to destruction. We let that secret sauce of our actions mature as we add various ingredients to either our pleasant surprise or disappointing demise. We make decisions as a nation or as individuals that will ultimately impact our spiritual outcomes, successes, and lasting Christian legacies. The totality of the if-then arrangement will play out on that God-given stage of life… His creation.

So the question must be asked. Will the if-then decisions in your life lead to a fine Italian sauce or one that is bitter and repugnant to the taste?

Finally, we see the collaborative nature of the two distinct forces. It is impossible to have one without the other. Outside of God Himself, an outcome cannot materialize without specific and actionable input from the human race. Both input and output work in tandem and in parallel, charting the spiritual graphs of life. They move in concert with one another. If the input (the "if") is man-focused and inherently evil, then the output (the "then") will be tainted with the evidences of this present world.

Some even may choose the path of compromise as the input (the "if") is straddled conveniently between the things of the Lord and the things of this present world. Once again, the output (the "then") assumes a position similar to that of the Church of Laodicea, a church that was comfortable being in a lukewarm state. In this example, God made it very clear what He thinks about compromise.

> "I know thy works, that thou art neither cold nor hot: I would thou wert cold or hot. So then because thou art lukewarm, and neither cold nor hot, I will spew thee out of my mouth." (Revelation 3:15-16)

If (and to the "praise of His glory") the input (the "if") is God-centered and motivated by the Spirit of God, then the output (the "then") will be covered by the life-giving blood of Jesus Christ, our Lord and Savior. We will then bask in the light of His glory and reach unknown spiritual heights according to His will. We serve a God of love who simply wants us to be obedient to His Word.

Will you join me today and determine that the if-then decisions in our lives will lead us to a clear path of serving an almighty God? Please pray with me to that end!

CHRISTIAN LEADERSHIP WORLDVIEW – PRINCIPLE #3

The decisions we make here on earth will leave an indelible mark on our friends, family, and other loved ones. Those decisions will allow us to leave a lasting legacy for future generations. We must thoughtfully and painstakingly render meaningful decisions for the glory of God.

4
EMBRACING GOD'S WORD

"The Bible is a revelation of the mind and will of God to men. Therein we may learn, what God is."
Jupiter Hammon

What are all of those key ingredients that make up the core elements of a *Christian leadership worldview*? That discussion can be both challenging and formidable. Let us consider for a moment that God has not only blessed us with a wonderful *Christian leadership worldview* roadmap in the Bible, He even has gone to great lengths to fill in all of the small and granular details as well. I truly believe that the Word of God is an expansive and comprehensive document for leadership.

While there is a host of good supplemental reading about Christian leadership, I have yet to encounter any useful teaching about leadership that cannot be traced back to the Word of God. Over time, many authors and well-intentioned folks simply have reframed, re-written, or re-communicated key Bible leadership principles. They have done so in ways that make Christian leadership principles relevant and understandable in today's culture. I am okay with that as long as the Bible is given full credit as the ultimate source when doctrinal standards are met.

I would like to challenge Christian leaders to think about all of those key leadership ingredients that make up a *Christian leadership worldview*. Here are a few things to consider, and I am sure that you have many more to share:

- We strive to exhibit the fruit of the Spirit as we draw closer to our Savior.

- Putting on the whole armor of God will equip us to fight the good fight and run the race that is set before us.
- When we are clothed in His righteousness and we put on the mind of Christ, we desire to serve Him and be true servant leaders.
- The charity and love of God constrains us to move beyond self for the good of other people with an unfathomable compassion.
- We take great thought to measure our conversations, decisions, and actions against the filter of God's Word.
- We *take action* with a "God consciousness" of our leadership responsibilities.
- We desire to have a *Christian leadership worldview* on purpose.
- When possible, our *Christian leadership worldview* should be geared toward higher levels of thinking that encompass "the big picture", along with deeper and broader concepts of intellectual and spiritual pursuits for the glory of God.
- We desire that our *Christian leadership worldview* will reach for the hope we have in Christ Jesus.
- We develop a clear vision of an eternity with Christ that will propel us to be willing instruments for His service today.

> **CHRISTIAN LEADERSHIP WORLDVIEW – PRINCIPLE #4**
>
> Thank you, Lord, for providing your Word to be my guide, allowing me to be the best possible leader that I can be. While I fall significantly short of my full leadership potential, I know that the Bible has made me a better leader. The Word of God has shown me what being a true leader is about. Christ is our servant leader example.

5
A LIVING SACRIFICE

"Faith is permitting ourselves to be seized by the things we do not see."
Martin Luther

We have all known for some time now that the spiritual and moral fiber of our country is deteriorating at an accelerating pace. Generally speaking, the things that Americans used to care about, rally around, and hold near and dear to their hearts are starting to fade into an oblivion of acceptance. The "you're-okay-and-I'm-okay" relativist mindset has made a dramatic impact on our culture. Does anyone really care anymore about fundamental Christianity?

As we continue to crunch the demographic profiles, slice the metadata, and aggressively survey our U.S. citizens, we start to understand what our national identity is becoming. In their article, "America's Changing Religious Landscape", the Pew Research Center detailed a significant number of religious trends that we need to be aware of and concerned about. The following survey results have been summarized from the Pew survey report:

- The Christian share of the U.S. population fell from 78.4% to 70.6% from 2007 to 2014.
- These declines are driven by mainstream Protestants and Catholics.
- Evangelical Christianity is falling at a slower rate (-0.9%). Some argue incorrectly that this fact is a good thing.
- Non-Christian faiths grew by 1.2% overall.
- Changes are taking place across all religious landscapes.

- All regions of the country and many demographic groups are being affected.
- The younger generation is less inclined to identify with a religious affiliation.[1]

With the Pew report as a backdrop, I would like to compare and contrast an authentic, passionate, active, and disciplined approach to fundamental Christianity against a term that I will label, "Pop Culture Christianity."

I believe that God has made it very clear what His expectations are for us here on earth. In Romans 12:1-2, the Bible states,

> "I beseech you therefore, brethren, by the mercies of God, that ye present your bodies a living sacrifice, holy, acceptable unto God, which is your reasonable service. And be not conformed to this world: but be ye transformed by the renewing of your mind, that ye may prove what is that good, and acceptable, and perfect, will of God."

Let's take a moment to unpack those two verses in *Romans* that are so rich with instruction for our daily living.

1. The Apostle Paul is **"beseeching"** the Christian brethren to take action. In other words, Paul is asking them urgently and fervently to do something. He is imploring, begging, entreating, and calling on them for action. This is not a "ho-hum" and "fly-under-the-radar-screen" type of request. This request is filled with a desire and passion for Christians to live in a specific and peculiar way.
2. Paul indicates it is by the **"mercies of God"** that we should act. He is reminding us that his pleading is

not coming through an expectation of human wisdom and intervention but that God in His mercy is sovereign and will intercede on our behalves through the guidance of the Holy Spirit.

3. Paul then throws down the gauntlet and gives us a clear "call to action" of the highest magnitude. We are to yield and present our **"bodies a living sacrifice."** The lesson here is that we were bought with a price. Christ died for our sins, and we were adopted into the family of God. We look to our Savior at the time when He walked the face of this earth as our example. We, too, should walk as Christ walked, living our lives as a sacrifice and testimony for the glory of God. As we present our bodies a living sacrifice, there is little room for concern with self. Rather, we selflessly look for opportunities to magnify and proclaim the name of Jesus. By definition and of necessity, a life of sacrifice must cost us something, or it would not be a valid representation of what it means to bow, yield, and submit.

4. Next, we see the words, **"Holy, acceptable unto God"**, as a condition of our sacrificial living. We are to consecrate, sanctify, and hallow our temple for the Master's use. We are to mortify our flesh. Yes, we must destroy that old, sin nature of our old man. In so doing, we are able to bring that Christ-likeness with all of its purity and righteousness to our way of living, a way of living that is spotless and sacrificial before our Lord.

5. At the end of the first verse, Paul uses the words, **"Which is your reasonable service."** This hit me like a sledge hammer as I was writing this chapter. Based on what the Savior was willing to endure in

order for us to be reconciled to the Father, it is the least that we can do. It is a justifiable and reasonable thing that Paul is suggesting based on Christ's sacrifice. If the God of this universe was willing to send His Son to this earth as 100-percent God and 100-percent man to die for the sins of mankind, it is reasonable that we should serve the Lord in a sacrificial capacity. There should be no second thoughts on this issue.

6. We are then told, "**And be not to be conformed to this world.**" We are not like the world, its system, and the "mixed multitude" among us. We should be a separate and peculiar people, a people who must be *in* the world but not *of* the world. We should be 100-percent different from the world. People should see Christ in us; should they not? If not, why not? As Christians, we need to be very careful about not living and developing a "pop culture" mentality. Clearly, that would be the easiest path to choose, one where we simply could get along with everyone, agree with everything they say, and ultimately stand for nothing. We eventually would come to the point where our Christian standards and values became unrecognizable.

7. Next, the verse tells us, "**But be ye transformed by the renewing of your mind.**" Transformation is a radical action and 360-degree change from its point of origin. This is not an incremental approach to the way we live our lives. This is not a checklist of works that allows us to gain favor with an Almighty God. This is a radical, spiritual awakening that should change who we are and our way of thinking. God has given to us the ability to renew our minds in a multitude of ways:

- Communion with Him through thoughtful and determined prayer
- Refreshment in His Word with daily Bible reading
- Praise and thankfulness for who He is and what He has done for us
- Meditation and solemn consideration of the whole counsel of God
- Preaching and teaching His Word
- Service and involvement in the lives of others through the use of our spiritual gifts
- Die daily to our old sin nature
- By faith, allowance of the Holy Spirit to direct our daily decisions
- See God in creation and His wonderful handiwork
- And the list goes on and on and on…

8. Lastly, the Apostle Paul writes, **"That ye may prove what is that good, and acceptable, and perfect, will of God."** As we strive to do the will of the Father through a life of sacrifice, we constantly are proving and working out our salvation unto the Lord. In our journey here on earth, we should be searching diligently for that perfect will of God, searching by means that are consistent with His holy and righteous nature. When we strive in this fashion, God ultimately honors us with those sought after words, "Well done, thy good and faithful servant."

Let's now juxtapose what we have just learned from the Apostle Paul about what a "living sacrifice" means as opposed to striving for a "pop culture" affinity and identity. Yes, I would argue that, if we are not seeking a God-centered existence, then we have bowed to the prince of this world and have purposed to identify with all that the world represents. It has been articulated many times before that there are only two choices on the shelf: You either serve God or you serve yourself.[2]

What does today's popular culture teach us about life, its significance, and the duties to which we are bound? Does any of this look familiar in today's popular culture?

- Individualism
- Manipulation
- Disrespectfulness
- Self-gratification
- Relativism
- Pleasure-seeking
- Non-conformist
- Anti-establishment
- Independence
- Prosperity-seeking
- Self-satisfaction

CALL TO ACTION

Let us tie the three main points of this chapter together. First, it is evident that we are losing our national Christian identity at an alarming rate. Second, the Bible articulates what our responsibilities are as ambassadors for Christ. Third, having a popular-culture identification is clearly at odds with God's character.

We are obligated to take up our spiritual arms and combat the forces of evil. We need to be activists in our Christian leadership endeavors and commit to a *Christian leadership worldview*. I am so thankful that I serve a God of action who was willing to come to this earth and up-end the traditional ways of thinking during that time period. We can't sit back and allow Satan and his minions to impact the world negatively. As Christians, we are called to have both dominion and stewardship responsibilities. We serve a powerful and mighty Lord! His expectations of us are quite formidable! Will you join me and make a difference today?

> **CHRISTIAN LEADERSHIP WORLDVIEW – PRINCIPLE #5**
>
> Jesus Christ wants us to be the salt of the earth. He wants us to fight against the moral and spiritual depravity that this world represents. We can do this by putting on the mind of Christ and not identifying with a popular culture that misses the mark spiritually. We have tremendous liberty in Christ, but it shouldn't be used as an occasion for the flesh. Praise God!

6

DEVELOPING OTHERS THROUGH COACHING

"A leader is one who knows the way, goes the way, and shows the way."
John C. Maxwell

As Christian leaders, we will have the privilege of making an impact on people's lives over the course of our lifetimes. Therefore, having a proper leadership coaching framework will help guide our thinking in this vital Christian training and development area. Below, is a practical, five-step leadership coaching model.

1. **Listen:** Leaders must teach those who they are coaching/mentoring what it means to adhere to wise counsel.
    - "Ointment and perfume rejoiceth the heart: so doth the sweetness of a man's friend by hearty counsel." (Proverbs 27:9)
    - "Without counsel purposes are disappointed: but in the multitude of counselors they are established." (Proverbs 15:22)
    - "Where no counsel is, the people fall: but in the multitude of counselors there is safety." (Proverbs 11:14)
    - "Iron sharpeneth iron; so a man sharpeneth the countenance of his friend." (Proverbs 27:17)

2. **Learn:** Leaders should formulate logical thought processes and core beliefs.
   - "Study to show thyself approved unto God, a workman that needeth not to be ashamed, rightly dividing the word of truth." (2 Timothy 2:15)
   - "Then I saw, and considered it well: I looked upon it, and received instruction." (Proverbs 24:32)
   - "For the commandment is a lamp; and the law is light; and reproofs of instruction are the way of life." (Proverbs 6:23)
   - "Apply thine heart unto instruction, and thine ears to the words of knowledge." (Proverbs 23:12)

3. **Let go:** Leaders then transition (by the leading of the Holy Spirit) toward a concern for the needs of others (servant leadership) and away from a "me-first" attitude.
   - "And he sat down, and called the twelve, and saith unto them, If any man desire to be first, the same shall be last of all, and servant of all." (Mark 9:35)
   - "Master, which is the great commandment in the law? Jesus said unto him, Thou shalt love the Lord thy God with all thy heart, and with all thy soul, and with all thy mind. This is the first and great commandment. And the second is like unto it, Thou shalt love thy neighbor as thyself. On these two commandments hang all the law and the prophets." (Matthew 22:36-40)

- "But so shall it not be among you: but whosoever will be great among you, shall be your minister: And whosoever of you will be the chiefest, shall be servant of all. For even the Son of man came not to be ministered unto, but to minister, and to give his life a ransom for many." (Mark 10:43-45)
- "If I then, your Lord and Master, have washed your feet; ye also ought to wash one another's feet. For I have given you an example, that ye should do as I have done to you. Verily, verily, I say unto you, The servant is not greater than his lord; neither he that is sent greater than he that sent him. If ye know these things, happy are ye if ye do them." (John 13:14-17)
- "Let another man praise thee, and not thine own mouth; a stranger, and not thine own lips." (Proverbs 27:2)

4. **Live:** Leaders use experiences and insight gained from the Word of God to live out a Christian Leadership Worldview.
    - "Through wisdom is a house builded; and by understanding it is established: And by knowledge shall the chambers be filled with all precious and pleasant riches." (Proverbs 24:3-4)
    - "For wisdom is the principle thing; therefore get wisdom: and with all thy getting get understanding." (Proverbs 4:7)
    - "The fruit of the righteous is a tree of life; and he that winneth souls is wise." (Proverbs 11:30)

- "Therefore whosoever heareth these sayings of mine, and doeth them, I will liken him unto a wise man, which built his house upon a rock:" (Matthew 7:24)

5. **Lead**: Take those lessons of life, and become the leader/mentor that God wants you to be.
    - "And Caleb stilled the people before Moses, and said, Let us go up at once, and possess it; for we are well able to overcome it." (Numbers 13:30)
    - "A good name is rather to be chosen than great riches, and loving favor rather than silver and gold." (Proverbs 22:1)
    - "Then the presidents and princes sought to find occasion against Daniel concerning the kingdom; but they could find none occasion or fault; forasmuch as he was faithful, neither was there any error or fault found in him." (Daniel 6:4)
    - "And Joshua the son of Nun was full of the spirit of wisdom; for Moses had laid his hands upon him: and the children of Israel hearkened unto him, and did as the Lord commanded Moses." (Deuteronomy 34:9)

5-STEP LEADERSHIP COACHING MODEL

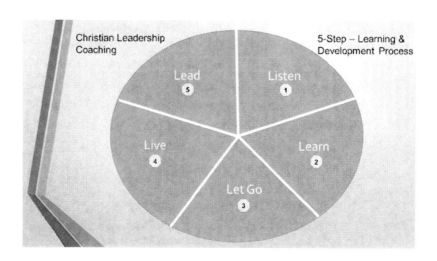

CORE LEADERSHIP COACHING ELEMENTS

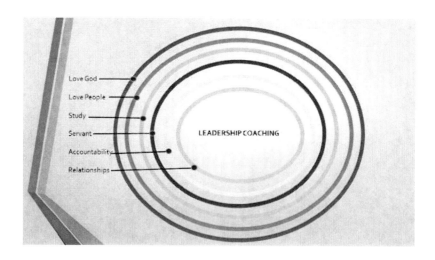

> **CHRISTIAN LEADERSHIP WORLDVIEW – PRINCIPLE #6**
>
> Leadership development spans a lifetime. Great leaders learn to become servants and listeners first. They are relationship builders who truly are concerned with the welfare of others. They tend to be diligent in all areas of life. They live and lead by example. Leadership coaches first invest in the spiritual development of their team members.

7

SURROUND YOURSELF WITH CHRISTIAN HEROES

"Associate with men of good quality if you esteem your own reputation;
for it is better to be alone than in bad company."
George Washington

It has been said often that if you want to understand the character of a man or a woman, just look at his or her inner circle of friends and those he or she looks up to. This is one of the most understated phrases of all time. Just think about it! Who you associate with has an enormous impact on your development and level of spiritual maturity.

Many people want to associate with, hang out with, and be around those who are just like them. They want to feel comfortable that what they say, how they dress, and what they do will be accepted within their immediate circles. In a sense, they are insulating themselves from potential criticism, reproof, insecurities, and the thought that what they have become as human beings may not measure up to the highest standards of thought, language, and behavior. In other words, they want to be left alone to be "who they are" while basking in spiritual mediocrity.

On the other hand and more positively stated, there are some who have chosen their Christian friends and associates very wisely. They have sought out individuals that have the ability to challenge and mentor them toward new levels of spiritual maturity and awareness. In my mind, those are the keepers. We should surround ourselves with friends who are disciplined, loving, and have a *Christian leadership worldview*. We should choose friends and confidants who will lift us up when we are down, remind us of our fallen state when we get "puffed up" in the flesh, and drive us toward Christ-like behavior patterns.

Please do not think for a minute that I am trying to create or propose a super-spiritual elite group of Christians who feel they are better than everyone else. Absolutely not! On the contrary, as "iron sharpeneth iron", we should be more willing than ever to involve ourselves in the lives of others. As we draw closer to the Savior, we should be willing to step out by faith (and out of our comfort zones) to do what may seem to be the impossible for Christ. This means building lasting relationships with both non-Christians and those in the faith that need additional spiritual encouragement. The bottom line is that we are called to make an impact on the world (people) with the gospel message.

Next, there are those in our lives who we look up to and admire. Many of these folks may not be part of our inner circle, but they seem to be squared away and have it all together from a Christian perspective. While they are sinners saved by the grace of God, there is something about them that we want to emulate. These Christians have been tried and tested on the battlefield for Christ. The Apostle Paul has a lot to say about those who we look up to and admire in the faith. He told the Philippians to "mark them" and imitate those among them that live out their faith in a Christ-like manner similar to himself.

> "Brethren, be followers together of me, and mark them which walk so as ye have us for an example. (For many walk, of whom I have told you often, and now tell you even weeping, that they are the enemies of the cross of Christ: Whose end is destruction, whose God is their belly, and whose glory is in their shame, who mind earthly things.)"
> (Philippians 3:17-19)

So let us recap just for a moment. First, we are to carefully and prayerfully surround ourselves with those individuals who will build us up in the faith. Second, we are to imitate those Christians who have proven to be spiritual giants. Third, we need to make sure we are making an impact on others for the cause of Christ. We need to be about our

Father's business and make sure we are ministering to and touching the lives of others.

We may look at Chapter 11 in the book of *Hebrews*, known as the "Hall of Faith", as a good starting point for learning about our Christian heroes.

By faith, Abel…
By faith, Enoch…
By faith, Noah…
By faith, Abraham…
Through faith also, Sarah…
By faith, Isaac…
By faith, Jacob…
By faith, Joseph…
By faith, Moses…

> "And what shall I more say? For the time would fail me to tell of Gideon, and of Barak, and of Samson, and of Jephthah; of David also, and Samuel, and of the prophets: Who through faith subdued kingdoms, wrought righteousness, obtained promises, stopped the mouths of lions, Quenched the violence of fire, escaped the edge of the sword, out of weakness were made strong, waxed valiant in fight, turned to flight the armies of the aliens."
> (Hebrews 11:32-34)

What a blessing it is to look to our Judeo-Christian forefathers as examples in the faith. Yes, sinfully, they were flawed men and women, but they desired to live by faith.

Then, we compare this prior list of Christian heroes of the faith to the pop culture icons of today, and we shake our heads in disbelief and dismay. Where is the spiritual depth?

We only can hope and pray that the Holy Spirit of God drives our country in a bright new direction. Please pray with me for a new spiritual direction and that our HEROES FOR LIFE once again become those Christian giants who are exemplary both in substance and in faith! Praise God!

Who are your heroes and those you want to be like?

CHRISTIAN LEADERSHIP WORLDVIEW – PRINCIPLE #7

Christians need to surround themselves with fellow believers that are strong in the faith. We need to "mark" those that have become Christian giants. Learning from those who are elders and are more spiritually mature is part of God's plan for the Church.

8
OBEDIENCE TO GOD'S CALL

"God is God. Because he is God, He is worthy of my trust and obedience. I will find rest nowhere but in His holy will that is unspeakably beyond my largest notions of what he is up to."
Elisabeth Elliot

The prodding, leading, and ultimate calling of the Holy Spirit can be challenging times in the life of a Christian. While as "new creatures in Christ" we should have a predisposition to spiritual and heavenly matters, it is not quite as simple as it sounds to follow our Master's leading. We are asked to step out by faith and enter into an environment where we are willing instruments for His service and good pleasure. Seems like an easy thing to accomplish. Right?

Just pick up and leave your friends, family (children, grandchildren), employer, and the routine of the familiar. Perhaps the Holy Spirit is directing you to another country, state, city, ministry, or an entirely new "comfort" zone. Please don't ask me to do that!

The story we see in the book of *Jonah* is played out time and again in the Old and New Testaments. God calls, and man runs for the hills. Sometimes, we question and debate with God about His calling for our lives. We think that the Lord must somehow be mistaken in His choice of vessels. *Impossible, he can't mean me!*

In Jonah 1:2, God called Jonah to the city of Nineveh, a magnificent city but one that was full of wickedness and the allure of self-gratification. Certainly, it was a city worthy of destruction. Jonah had no desire to preach the gospel message in a city where they did not know right from wrong.

The undeniable stench of sin wafting to God's nostrils prompted God to act!

> "Arise, go to Nineveh, that great city, and cry against
> it; for their wickedness is come up before me."
> (Jonah 1:2)

So Jonah in the perfect form of human weakness and frailty decided to run! Not only did he run, but he almost ran in the opposite direction from where the Lord wanted him to serve and minister.

> "But Jonah rose up to flee unto Tarshish from the
> presence of the Lord, and went down to Joppa; and
> he found a ship going to Tarshish: so he paid the
> fare thereof, and went down into it, to go with them
> unto Tarshish from the presence of the Lord."
> (Jonah 1:3)

Well, you know the rest of the story. God called a second time, and Jonah heeded the calling after a little debacle with a fish (whale).

> "So Jonah arose, and went unto Nineveh, according
> to the word of the Lord. Now Nineveh was an ex-
> ceeding great city of three days journey."
> (Jonah 3:3)

We see a similar example played out in the leadership calling of Moses. God called Moses to lead the nation of Israel out of Egypt. Moses had a totally different perspective on the issue.

> "And Moses said unto God, Who am I, that I
> should go unto Pharaoh, and that I should bring
> forth the children of Israel out of Egypt?"
> (Exodus 3:11)

> "And Moses said unto God, Behold, when I come
> unto the children of Israel, and shall say unto them,

The God of your fathers hath sent me unto you; and they shall say to me, What is his name? What shall I say unto them?" (Exodus 3:13)

"And Moses answered and said, But, behold, they will not believe me, nor hearken unto my voice: for they will say, The Lord hath not appeared unto thee." (Exodus 4:1)

"And Moses said unto the Lord, O my Lord, I am not eloquent, neither therefore, nor since thou hast spoken unto thy servant: but I am slow of speech, and of a slow tongue." (Exodus 4:10)

"And Moses returned unto the Lord, and said, Lord, wherefore hast thou so evil entreated this people? Why is it that thou hast sent me?"
(Exodus 5:22)

"And Moses spake before the Lord, saying, Behold, the children of Israel have not hearkened unto me; how then shall Pharaoh hear me, who am of uncircumcised lips?" (Exodus 6:12)

"And Moses said before the Lord, Behold, I am of uncircumcised lips, and how shall Pharaoh hearken unto me?" (Exodus 6:30)

"And Moses cried unto the Lord, saying, What shall I do unto this people? They be almost ready to stone me." (Exodus 17:4)

So that leads me back to a question for self-examination. *What is your Nineveh?* Are you running or questioning some things that God has asked you to do? Are you purposefully and knowingly running in the opposite direction from where God wants you? Are you avoiding the issue of full-time service? How about making a decision to serve our risen Savior?

For me, the word *Nineveh* represents a choice, a choice of life-long service to God or to self. Ultimately, both Moses and Jonah accepted the gift and the calling from above. Will you? What is your *Nineveh*?

CHRISTIAN LEADERSHIP WORLDVIEW – PRINCIPLE #8

Believers need to be in tune with the prompting and leading of the Holy Spirit. They also need to be confident when God calls them to a particular ministry that they are the perfect and chosen vessel for that specific opportunity to serve. Don't gauge your calling by whether or not you feel inadequate or unworthy. Simply be willing to give it your all when God asks you to serve. By the way, He *will* ask.

9

BE SILENT BEFORE HIM

> *"It becomes us in humility to make our devout acknowledgments to the*
> *Supreme Ruler of the Universe for the inestimable civil and*
> *religious blessings with which we are favored."*
> ***James K. Polk***

I lift up my prayers and come boldly
to the throne of His imminent grace.
You tell me it's there I will find You,
Christ Jesus, the High Potentate.

To enter the realm of His presence,
past sin is left at the door.
My Savior is the Holy One.
This temple did He restore.

Christ says He wants our obedience.
Prostrate before Him is all,
stretched-out-ed-ly seeking the Master,
expectantly heeding His call.

To the Lord, we give all thanksgiving,
raised hands with joyful praise,
never forgetting His wonderful love.
This life on earth has He made.

Jehovah invites us to join Him
to commune with Him all the day long,
that still small place He created,
with hymns and spiritual songs.

To learn to pray without ceasing,
a marvelous, wonderful gift.
A disciplined life, all devotion to Him,
supplications and prayers do we lift.

Taking stock of His Kingdom around us,
being silent before Him we must
with worship and adoration,
in this Savior, we place our great trust.

CHRISTIAN LEADERSHIP WORLDVIEW – PRINCIPLE #9

This poem was written to express the holy and righteous nature of our majestic God in relation to our responsibilities as humble servants before Him. When we are in His presence, there should be a real sense of who Christ is and who we are as sinners saved by the grace of God. The relationship is one where we can do nothing else but bow before Him in a position of utter and total dependence.

When we commune with Jesus through our prayers, we are reminded of a Father who dearly loves us and wants the best for His children, a Father who is the Master and Sovereign of His domain with little children submitting and yielding to His will for our lives. We yield because of the wonderful work of salvation that was wrought in us by a mighty God, so powerful that He created the universe and sent His Son, Jesus Christ, to die on the cross of Calvary for the sins of mankind. We praise Him and shout hallelujah for our Creator, Redeemer, and Friend!

10

SUFFICIENCY IN CHRIST

> *"We should always look upon ourselves as God's servants, placed in God's world, to do his work; and accordingly labour faithfully for him; not with a design to grow rich and great, but to glorify God, and do all the good we possibly can."*
> *David Brainerd*

Do you remember the day when you graduated from high school or college with an incredible sense of freedom along with a desire and longing to be all on your own? There may have been an excitement in the air with the thought of setting out to chart a path in life that was considered "all yours." As you contemplated those life issues, you thought to yourself that you had the ability, wherewithal, and good common sense to make a unique and indelible impact on others, perhaps even on people halfway around the world. There were so many plans to make and questions to ponder. You may have thought, "What impact will I make? What kind of legacy will I leave for future generations? What can I achieve in the next five, ten, or fifteen years? How far will I progress in my career? Will I be the president or vice president of a major corporation? Will I get married? How many children will I have? Where will we live?" These thoughts and others probably were accompanied with exhilarating emotion along with an eager anticipation to know what the future might hold for your life.

But one thing was for sure; you felt ready for the task at hand. "The challenge will be met head on!" you exclaimed. "I can do it! I will be on my own and will conquer the world," you thought. While your parents may have provided an adequate or even a wonderful environment for your upbringing and may have done a terrific job in the parenting department, there was just that romantic thought of being your own man or woman. More than likely, your parents diligently and painstakingly taught you the rules of the road for that purpose we call "life." They sacrificed their time, energy, and finances so that you would be equipped to make it in that "big bad world" out there.

As you got older and became ready to head out to meet those challenges of life, your parents may have jokingly quipped, "My children are all off the family payroll now and are making it on their own." Isn't that the heart's desire of most parents? They want to see their children grow up to be self-sufficient.

How long did it take for your children to become self-sufficient? How long did it take you? Are you self-sufficient right now?

If your answer to the last question above is "no", then you might be on the right track. You may have come to the conclusion and have the depth of character and spiritual understanding to know that, as a child of God, you will never be self-sufficient outside of His wonderful grace.

Yes, it is a good thing to work hard, provide a living for our families, and pay our bills. Generally speaking, we should not look to others to support our families (barring extreme and unusual circumstances) or feel entitled to ongoing support that is not earned, regardless of what the world might be telling us. And, yes, there may be times when reaching down to provide a helping Christian hand to others is needed and a blessing from above. However, in the long-haul, God has designed man to work and provide for his family. That is a biblical mandate and a God-given principle.

We must also remember that God has designed the human race in a way that social interaction and reliance on powers greater than ourselves (Christ) are paramount for successful living. We are to nurture and develop those horizontal covenant relationships with fellow believers. We should care for, minister to, and provide spiritual encouragement to one another as part of who we are as Christians. That should be our *Christian leadership worldview*. God has created man in His image, and followers of Christ have the indwelling of the Holy Spirit. Therefore, we should strive to be thoughtful and considerate of others before ourselves. Christ was the epitome of relying on His Heavenly Father for sufficiency. Christ's example of servant leadership is a well-known fact among Christians and non-Christians alike.

Quite frankly, self-sufficiency is at the opposite end of the spectrum in Christendom. We should want our children to rely on other Christians (for accountability) and to develop a worldview that seeks the sufficiency of our Lord and Savior, Jesus Christ. We are taught in God's Word to be totally and utterly dependent on the Heavenly Father. The expression, "more of Him and less of me", is an appropriate tagline. There is no weakness in relying on the Savior for our daily needs. The Word of God gives us wonderful and detailed instruction on the topic of sufficiency in Christ.

The three verses below sum up quite nicely our responsibility to embrace our Savior for the sufficiency that we require here on God's created earth. The Bible teaches us not to think too highly of ourselves and become self-sufficient and self-reliant but rather to embrace the gift of grace that is provided through a personal and loving relationship with Jesus Christ. He will provide all of our earthly and heavenly needs. We are to rest in Him. It is an awe-inspiring message that is full of grace, hope, redemption, and reliance on the King of Kings and Lord of Lords!

> "Not that we are sufficient of ourselves to think anything as of ourselves; but our sufficiency is of God; Who also hath made us able ministers of the new testament; not of the letter, but of the Spirit: for the letter killeth, but the spirit giveth life."
> (2 Corinthians 3:5-6)

> "And he said unto me, My grace is sufficient for thee: for my strength is made perfect in weakness. Most gladly therefore will I rather glory in my infirmities, that the power of Christ may rest upon me."
> (2 Corinthians 12:9)

The Bible also gives us great warning about self-sufficiency. We are to flee the old, sin nature of self. Ultimately, we will reap what we sow and suffer the consequences. The reality of this message is servitude and punishment as we yield our members to sin rather than yielding to an Almighty God.

> "But thou didst trust in thine own beauty, and playedst the harlot because of thy renown, and pouredst out thy fornications on everyone that passed by; his it was." (Ezekiel 16:15)

> "And they made a calf in those days, and offered sacrifice unto the idol, and rejoiced in the works of their own hands." (Acts 7:41)

> "But they refused to hearken, and pulled away the shoulder, and stopped their ears, that they should not hear." (Zechariah 7:11)

> "And when ye did eat, and when ye did drink, did not ye eat for yourselves, and drink for yourselves?" (Zechariah 7:6)

> "For because thou hast trusted in thy works and in thy treasures, thou shalt also be taken: and Chemosh shall go forth into captivity with his priests and his princes together." (Jeremiah 48:7)

What are you trusting in today? Who are you relying on? Are you trusting in your own strength to navigate this dying and wicked world? Are you trying to conquer the mountaintops all on your own? Or is your sufficiency in Christ and Christ alone? Does the question, "Are you self-sufficient?" tug at your heart strings?

> **CHRISTIAN LEADERSHIP WORLDVIEW – PRINCIPLE #10**
>
> This chapter was written as a companion to another chapter titled, "The Me Generation." My prayer is that these two chapters will be a blessing and will challenge you to put greater trust, reliance, and faith in the One who matters: Christ. We become stronger when we let go and allow Christ to be our sufficiency. This, too, is one of the beautiful paradoxes of the Christian faith. There is great strength in weakness! Amen!

Part 2
The Fundamentals of Organizational Leadership

11
PROJECT MANAGEMENT 101

"Honor bespeaks worth. Confidence begets trust. Service brings satisfaction. Cooperation proves the quality of leadership."
James Cash Penney

Dear Friend, I would like to tell you a story about an amazing man, a man who had the passion, drive, and sheer willpower to tackle a most formidable project. Like many of us, this man had an "employer" who had assigned to him one of the most daring and incomprehensible feats one could ever imagine.

We've all experienced something like this before. Haven't we? Someone at work or at home challenges us with some chore or project that seems impossible. We think to ourselves, "There is just no way this is going to happen... No way!"

This particular man happened to be employed by, indentured to, a prisoner of, and a humble servant of the Lord our God. This man's anchor was firmly grounded and attached to a Father who resides in heaven above.

Let me tell you a little about this individual. Let's explore his character, motivation, and how he went about completing his assigned project. After reading down through some of these one-word descriptions, can you guess who it is? Can you guess who was blessed with such God-given abilities?

Discernment	Trust	Trustworthiness	Planning	Vision
Persuasion	Delegation	Persistence	Determination	Political
Caring	Leader	Prayerful	Integrity	Love
Unselfishness	Resilient	Execution	Completion	Detail
Organizer	Godly	Brave	Faith	

Okay, I know what you're thinking. It could be a host of characters from the Bible. Let me give you a little clue. The clue is "52 days." It took this talented man 52 days to lead the completion of what God had commissioned him to do, a most improbable feat. Remember that God is in control of our lives and our circumstances. In the face of ominous and daunting conditions, we must trust in the Lord and allow Him to rule our lives.

Yes, I am referring to the biblical account of how Nehemiah led the rebuilding of the walls of Jerusalem in a very short period of time. I would like to recount the godly wisdom that Nehemiah exhibited as he motivated the people of Jerusalem to inspiring heights. I believe that this "Project Management 101" account has key learning information for us today. If we would apply some of the principles in this article to projects we are now tackling, how successful could we be? By using many of these same principles, could we be better servant leaders and employees, thus improving our overall efficiency and results? There is so much application for the workplace, church ministries, nonprofits, and even projects in the home if we would take the time to unpack and discern the totality of Nehemiah's project management approach.

Let us now take a look at the series of steps Nehemiah took that ultimately led to a finished and successful project. These steps are not in any particular order, but I believe they capture the essence of his approach.

NEHEMIAH'S BURDEN

First, I believe that any and all project management assignments must start with the passion, burden, and desire to get things done. Nehemiah had such a burden for both the people of Israel and the reconstruction of the walls of Jerusalem.

> "And it came to pass, when I heard these words, that I sat down and wept, and mourned certain days, and fasted, and prayed before the God of heaven. And said, I beseech thee, O Lord God of heaven, the great and terrible God, that keepeth covenant and mercy for them that love him and observe his commandments." (Nehemiah 1:4)

NEHEMIAH'S SPIRITUAL INSIGHT

Next, the depth and breadth of his spiritual insight were enormous. Not only did Nehemiah have a burden for his people and the reconstruction of the wall, but God gave him spiritual discernment and understanding. Nehemiah had a deep comprehension of the prevailing issues and problems of the day.

In project management circles, problem identification and understanding is fundamental to moving forward. The issues need to be studied and analyzed from a variety of different angles. Project leaders must first understand what they are dealing with before they can offer concrete and sustainable solutions. Nehemiah knew that the nation of Israel was apostate in its actions and thoughts.

> "We have dealt very corruptly against thee, and have not kept the commandments, nor the statutes, nor the judgments, which thou commandedst thy servant Moses." (Nehemiah 1:7)

Nehemiah's Trust in God

While the circumstances of the day tended to be man-focused rather than God-centered, Nehemiah still trusted in God's promises. He believed that, if the people of Israel would turn back to God, great things would happen. Nehemiah understood that God fulfills His promises.

> "Remember, I beseech thee, the word that thou commandedst thy servant Moses, saying, If ye transgress, I will scatter you abroad among the nations. But if ye turn unto me, and keep my commandments, and do them; though there were of you cast out unto the uttermost part of the heaven, yet will I gather them from thence, and will bring them unto the place that I have chosen to set my name there. Now these are thy servants and thy people, whom thou hast redeemed by thy great power, and by thy strong hand." (Nehemiah 1:8-10)

Nehemiah's Trustworthiness

The stature and character of Nehemiah is also evident as he reached a position of prominence in the king's court. Nehemiah was the cupbearer for King Artaxerxes. This position was not easily obtained. It was a position that commanded the ultimate respect and trust of the king. Just think of the skill sets needed to rise to this level of trust within the king's inner circle. Pretty impressive!

> "O Lord, I beseech thee, let thine ear be attentive to the prayer of thy servant, and to the prayer of thy servants, who desire to fear thy name: and prosper, I pray thee, thy servant this day, and grant him mercy in the sight of this man. For I was the king's cupbearer." (Nehemiah 1:11)

NEHEMIAH'S RELATIONSHIP-BUILDING SKILLS

This next portion of scripture is very important to a project management understanding and focus. Nehemiah had the unique skill set to build deep and long-term relationships. He had built such a close bond with the king that he recognized when Nehemiah's countenance was downcast. He was not just another servant to the king. It is apparent that he meant something special to both the king and queen. The ability to build relationships is a vital skill in successful project management.

> "And it came to pass in the month Nisan, in the twentieth year of Artaxerxes the king, that wine was before him: and I took up the wine, and gave it unto the king. Now I had not been beforetime sad in his presence. Wherefore the king said unto me, Why is thy countenance sad, seeing thou art not sick? this is nothing else but sorrow of heart. Then I was very sore afraid, And said unto the king, Let the king live for ever: why should not my countenance be sad, when the city, the place of my fathers' sepulchres, lieth in waste, and the gates thereof are consumed with fire? Then the king said unto me, For what dost thou make request? So I prayed to the God of heaven. And I said unto the king, If it please the king, and if thy servant have found favor in thy sight, that thou wouldest send me unto Judah, unto the city of my fathers' sepulchres, that I may build it." (Nehemiah 2:1-5)

NEHEMIAH'S POLITICAL ASTUTENESS

In the following portion of scripture, his planning and maneuvering from a political perspective is clearly evident. He knew that there were "players" back in Jerusalem that would not be happy with what he was about to undertake. He wanted to make sure that everyone understood that King Artaxerxes was solidly on board and supported the mission. Nehemiah was also trying to create a clear path to success by leveraging all of the political capital he had developed with the king. Whether friend or foe back home in Jerusalem, Nehemiah wanted to make sure that everyone was in compliance with what he was attempting to accomplish. In other words, he wanted to remove any and all barriers to the successful completion of the wall.

When we practice successful project management in our respective organizations, aren't we trying to remove the barriers and create the enabling processes for success?

> "Moreover I said unto the king, If it please the king, let letters be given me to the governors beyond the river, that they may convey me over till I come into Judah; And a letter unto Asaph the keeper of the king's forest, that he may give me timber to make beams for the gates of the palace which appertained to the house, and for the wall of the city, and for the house that I shall enter into. And the king granted me, according to the good hand of my God upon me." (Nehemiah 2:7-8)

Nehemiah's Planning Abilities

Nehemiah was also blessed with exceptional planning skills. He understood what a project of this magnitude would require from a planning perspective. He knew that he could not just show up in Jerusalem and start rebuilding the wall. There had to be meticulous planning and forethought prior to the project's commencement. He needed to get a bird's-eye view of the task at hand.

Before we jump right into an assigned project at work or in the ministry, how much time should we spend deeply contemplating the task that is before us?

> "So I came to Jerusalem, and was there three days. And I arose in the night, I and some few men with me; neither told I any man what my God had put in my heart to do at Jerusalem: neither was there any beast with me, save the beast that I rode upon. And I went out by night by the gate of the valley, even before the dragon well, and to the dung port, and viewed the walls of Jerusalem, which were broken down, and the gates thereof were consumed with fire. Then I went on to the gate of the fountain, and to the king's pool: but there was no place for the beast that was under me to pass. Then went I up in the night by the brook, and viewed the wall, and turned back, and entered by the gate of the valley, and so returned." (Nehemiah 2:11-15)

NEHEMIAH'S PERSUASION

Great leaders and project managers have the ability to persuade. They have a special talent that allows them to create a vision for the people and get them excited and passionate for a cause. Nehemiah demonstrated this ability as can be seen in the portion of scripture above. What is so special about his persuasive abilities and approach is that he related it all back to God. Nehemiah believed that God must be at the forefront of this project for it to succeed. He wanted to make sure that everyone understood that God was directing his paths in this matter. He wasn't some power-hungry nutcase going this alone. He was motivated by the hand of God along with the king's blessing! It clearly had its intended effect.

> "Then said I unto them, Ye see the distress that we are in, how Jerusalem lieth waste, and the gates thereof are burned with fire: come, and let us build

up the wall of Jerusalem, that we be no more a reproach. Then I told them of the hand of my God which was good upon me; as also the king's words that he had spoken unto me. And they said, Let us rise up and build. So they strengthened their hands for this good work." (Nehemiah 2:17-18)

Nehemiah's Delegation of Assignments

In this passage, we see a division-of-work approach that included specific project assignments being delegated to various individuals and families. Everyone had a role that they would play in the construction of the wall. This is classic, *project management 101* kind of stuff. You create a vision, assign responsibilities, and then hold the people accountable for the results. The entire chapter of Nehemiah 3 is dedicated to the assignment of work.

Nehemiah Overcoming Adversity

Have you ever been in the middle of an important project, and everything went wrong? Perhaps you had a project to complete in which not everyone was on board. In the extreme, there may have been those who were trying to derail and completely sabotage your efforts. I think this happens more times than we would care to admit—if not in whole, at least, in part. For example, people may not quite be buying into your concept or what you are selling, and they maliciously try to take the project in an entirely new direction. In the corporate world, power struggles and jealousy issues happen all the time.

Well, Nehemiah faced this exact predicament. There were those completely opposed to rebuilding the wall, and they did everything they could to make it fail.

What will you do when adversity strikes? Will you succumb to the pressures of this world and abandon what you once thought was a God-given focus and passion? Or, will you pray and fight through the adversity, knowing that it is God's will for you to continue?

Let's visit a few portions of the Bible relating to Nehemiah overcoming adversity and how he handled it.

> "But it came to pass, that when Sanballat heard that we builded the wall, he was wroth, and took great indignation, and mocked the Jews. And he spake before his brethren and the army of Samaria, and said, What do these feeble Jews? will they fortify themselves? will they sacrifice? will they make an end in a day? will they revive the stones out of the heaps of the rubbish which are burned?"
> (Nehemiah 4:1-2)

> "And conspired all of them together to come and to fight against Jerusalem, and to hinder it."
> (Nehemiah 4:8)

николаевNEHEMIAH'S PRAYER

We know from the Bible that Nehemiah was a man of prayer. When adversity hit, he decided to pray. He was not a quitter. He knew that God had given to him a special commission and was going to see it through to the end. Nehemiah then did what he knew best. He prayed. Time and again, we see this man go to the God of this universe in earnest and heartfelt prayer. Nehemiah knew that he needed the Lord's guidance and intercession.

> "Hear, O our God; for we are despised: and turn their reproach upon their own head, and give them for a prey in the land of captivity: And cover not their iniquity, and let not their sin be blotted out

from before thee: for they have provoked thee to anger before the builders." (Nehemiah 4:4-5)

"Nevertheless we made our prayer unto our God, and set a watch against them day and night, because of them." (Nehemiah 4:9)

Nehemiah's Risk Mitigation

There were points in the construction of the wall when Nehemiah had to put plans in place to protect the people from physical harm and potential death. He took the necessary steps to mitigate the physical risk.

There are a couple of points I would like for us to consider relating to risk in a project management environment.

First, while people on our project teams may not be in physical danger, we still need to protect our employees. People who work for us on a project must know that it is okay to try new things, take risks, and even fail. They must know that their boss has their back and will stand up for them, provided they are doing all the right things.

Second, as project leaders, we are always scanning the environment to consider potential risk. Having a good risk management policy and considering overall risk must be an ongoing part of any and all project management initiatives.

"Therefore set I in the lower places behind the wall, and on the higher places, I even set the people after their families with their swords, their spears, and their bows." (Nehemiah 4:13)

Nehemiah's Motivation and Encouragement

Through the tough times of any project, the great leaders and managers always come through with words of motivation and encouragement. The great ones seem to know exactly what we need and when we need it.

They have this intuitive understanding and sense of when to encourage, confront, and motivate.

Think about the last time someone gave you some kind words of encouragement as you were working through a very difficult assignment. How did it make you feel? My guess is that it motivated you to want to do even more.

> "And I looked, and rose up, and said unto the nobles, and to the rulers, and to the rest of the people, Be ye not afraid of them: remember the Lord, which is great and terrible, and fight for your brethren, your sons, and your daughters, your wives, and your houses." (Nehemiah 4:14)

NEHEMIAH'S LEADERSHIP

I believe that Nehemiah was a true leader. He exhibited the qualities that inspire and motivate others to accomplish things they thought were impossible. He had a special gift to coordinate a diverse group of personalities around a common goal, mission, or project. Nehemiah's project management skills united the laborers to be of a mind to work.

> "So built we the wall; and all the wall was joined together unto the half thereof: for the people had a mind to work." (Nehemiah 4:6)

NEHEMIAH'S DETERMINATION

Like every good project leader, Nehemiah had an unparalleled determination to see the completion of the wall. Simply put, he was relentless in his pursuit and focus. With physical danger and harm on all sides, his project team showed a toughness to see it through. It was a labor of love, and nothing was going to get in their way.

> "They which builded on the wall, and they that bare burdens, with those that laded, every one with one of his hands wrought in the work, and with the other hand held a weapon." (Nehemiah 4:17)

> "So neither I, nor my brethren, nor my servants, nor the men of the guard which followed me, none of us put off our clothes, saving that every one put them off for washing." (Nehemiah 4:23)

NEHEMIAH'S INTEGRITY

Throughout chapter 5 in the book of *Nehemiah*, we also see clear examples of his integrity on display. Integrity is another character trait that must be part of one's personal makeup if one is ever going to be an effective project team leader. People must be able to trust the person that is leading them. Without integrity, there is no trust.

In the example below, Nehemiah was confronting his brethren about the tactic of charging "usury" to the poor and less fortunate. This business practice was forbidden under the Old Testament law. There were several other difficult situations like this that cropped up during the building of the wall that Nehemiah had to confront. There was also a famine going on at this time. Many of the laborers had no food, and they were forced to mortgage their land. Nehemiah confronted the misdeeds of the nobles and encouraged them to do the right thing according to his godly example.

> "And I was very angry when I heard their cry and these words. Then I consulted with my self, and I rebuked the nobles, and the rulers, and said unto them, Ye exact usury, every one of his brother. And I set a great assembly against them. And I said unto them, We after our ability have redeemed our brethren the Jews, which were sold unto the heathen; and

will ye even sell your brethren? or shall they be sold unto us? Then held they their peace, and found nothing to answer." (Nehemiah 5:6-8)

NEHEMIAH'S TOUGH LOVE

Sometimes, as project leaders, we are put in situations where we have to practice the art of "tough love." While this approach should be the choice of last resort, it must be shrouded in a spirit of love. Confrontation and giving direction is a fact of life. Bottom line: If you shy away from these types of situations, you will not be an effective project manager. In other words, in some specific instances, you will need to tell it like it is and expect compliance.

For Nehemiah, it was about much more than practicing "tough love" and telling others how to live up to Old Testament responsibilities. He walked the talk. Nehemiah tried to encourage the Jewish laborers to follow his example and to do the right thing. He wanted them to know how he had conducted himself concerning financial matters. He ultimately wanted them to know that his reliance was on God and not man.

> "Also I said, It is not good that ye do: ought ye not to walk in the fear of our God because of the reproach of the heathen our enemies? I likewise, and my brethren, and my servants, might exact of them money and corn: I pray you, let us leave off this usury. Restore, I pray you, to them, even this day, their lands, their vineyards, their oliveyards, and their houses, also the hundredth part of the money, and of the corn, the wine, and the oil, that ye exact of them." (Nehemiah 5:9-11)

Nehemiah's Unselfishness

> "Moreover from the time that I was appointed to be their governor in the land of Judah, from the twentieth year even unto the two and thirtieth year of Artaxerxes the king, that is, twelve years, I and my brethren have not eaten the bread of the governor. But the former governors that had been before me were chargeable unto the people, and had taken of them bread and wine, beside forty shekels of silver; yea, even their servants bare rule over the people: but so did not I, because of the fear of God."
> (Nehemiah 5:14-15)

Nehemiah's Generosity and Compassion

We can see further evidences of the character of Nehemiah through his generosity and compassion for others. He had a heart that was willing to give when he saw a need.

As a project management leader, how much are you willing to give for your team to be successful? Maybe your giving is not in monetary terms but with your time, encouragement, and front-line involvement. Maybe your giving as a project management leader is about being available for consultation, team building, and direction. It could be that you need to come down from "the ivory tower" and be among the people. Just getting to know them is probably one of the biggest and most generous gifts of all.

> "Moreover there were at my table a hundred and fifty of the Jews and rulers, beside those that came unto us from among the heathen that are about us. Now that which was prepared for me daily was one ox and six choice sheep; also fowls were prepared for me, and once in ten days store of all sorts of wine:

> yet for all this required not I the bread of the governor, because the bondage was heavy upon this people. Think upon me, my God, for good, according to all that I have done for this people."
> (Nehemiah 5:17-19)

NEHEMIAH'S DISCERNMENT

Project leaders must be able to demonstrate wisdom and discernment during the duration of a project. They must be able to understand the meaning of what is being said along with the underlying motivations of the key individuals. In other words, you must become proficient at reading between the lines. People and circumstances will not always be what they seem. There are times when the people you are working with have ulterior motives. Good project leaders always have their antennas up. This is not to say that you should go into every situation with a pessimistic or a negative situational analysis. You just need to remain in a state of awareness.

> "That Sanballat and Geshem sent unto me, saying, Come, let us meet together in some one of the villages in the plain of Ono. But they thought to do me mischief. And I sent messengers unto them, saying, I am doing a great work, so that I cannot come down: why should the work cease, whilest I leave it, and come down to you?" (Nehemiah 6:2-3)

NEHEMIAH BEING PERSECUTED

As Christians, we must be aware of and expect persecution. It is a shame that in the United States of America—where *toleration* is preached and is the rallying cry for many in our country—we need to be on-guard for those who would do us harm because of our religious beliefs. It may be very subtle and within the confines of the law, but chances are that your

Christian leadership worldview identity will bother some people, and you will come under attack. Christ made it very clear in His Word that, if you are a Christian, you will be persecuted. Again, I encourage you not to take a defeatist position and think that everyone is out to get you. Just be on guard and in a state of awareness.

In the first few verses below, Nehemiah was being accused of building the wall for the purpose of helping the Jews to rebel against their king. Later on, there was an attempt on his life.

> "Then sent Sanballat his servant unto me in like manner the fifth time with an open letter in his hand; Wherein was written, It is reported among the heathen, and Gashmu saith it, that thou and the Jews think to rebel: for which cause thou buildest the wall, that thou mayest be their king, according to these words." (Nehemiah 6:5-6)

> "Afterward I came unto the house of Shemaiah the son of Delaiah the son of Mehetabeel, who was shut up; and he said, Let us meet together in the house of God, within the temple, and let us shut the doors of the temple, for they will come to slay thee; yea, in the night will they come to slay thee. And I said, Should such a man as I flee? and who is there, that, being as I am, would go into the temple to save his life? I will not go in. And, lo, I perceived that God had not sent him; but that he pronounced this prophecy against me: for Tobiah and Sanballat had hired him." (Nehemiah 6:10-12)

NEHEMIAH FINISHED THE TASK

After all the trials and tribulation of leading his project team, Nehemiah finally began to see the light and draw his project initiative to a conclusion. He stuck in there and made sure that the project was finished. It took Nehemiah's project team 52 days to complete the work. What an example of teamwork! It goes to show what can be accomplished when one is able to harness the power of collective thought, hard work, dedication, and vision.

> "So the wall was finished in the twenty and fifth day of the month Elul, in fifty and two days."
> (Nehemiah 6:15)

SUMMARY

Let us take a moment to recap some of the important principles of project management that we can learn from Nehemiah's account. These principles are as relevant today as they were back in Old Testament times. I believe that these principles are the backbone and foundation to any successful project. Christians would do well to adhere to Nehemiah's "Project Management 101" principles.

- Nehemiah's Burden
- Nehemiah's Spiritual Insight
- Nehemiah's Trust in God
- Nehemiah's Trustworthiness
- Nehemiah's Relationship-Building Skills
- Nehemiah's Political Astuteness
- Nehemiah's Planning Abilities
- Nehemiah's Persuasion
- Nehemiah's Delegation of Assignments
- Nehemiah Overcoming Adversity
- Nehemiah's Prayer

- Nehemiah's Risk Mitigation
- Nehemiah's Motivation and Encouragement
- Nehemiah's Leadership
- Nehemiah's Determination
- Nehemiah's Integrity
- Nehemiah's Tough Love
- Nehemiah's Unselfishness
- Nehemiah's Generosity and Compassion
- Nehemiah's Discernment
- Nehemiah Being Persecuted
- Nehemiah Finished the Task

Dear Friend, I hope you have enjoyed the story of this godly man, Nehemiah, who brought a project team together and led them to victory despite what seemed to be insurmountable conditions. His faith, character, and wisdom allowed him to accomplish the impossible. We, too, can accomplish the impossible through our Lord and Savior, Jesus Christ.

What will your next project design look like?

CHRISTIAN LEADERSHIP WORLDVIEW – PRINCIPLE #11

When Christians face what seem to be insurmountable conditions in the workplace, look to the Bible for answers. When the complexities of the workplace seem to be much more than what we can handle, search the scriptures for examples of how we are to respond in the moment. Yes, God has even laid out a design for the workplace that we can benefit from. The secrets of organizational behavior are available in the Bible for our instruction.

12

THE QUIGLEY &
THE DISCIPLINED LEADER

By Kyle LaPierre

> *"When placed in command, take charge."*
> *Norman Schwarzkopf*

The Quigley and the combat course described in the anecdote below shouldn't be viewed as an evil or something we should try to avoid. Instead, it is part of the training a U.S. Marine must go through to come out stronger and to grow. In the same way, God puts trials in our lives that are for our own good. While we might not appreciate or enjoy the trials as we are going through them, we need to sit back and try to understand their spiritual significance. He wants us to become better Christian warriors and Christian leaders.

Likewise, we've been blessed with the tools to succeed. God is with us, but at the end of the day, God has given to us a choice. The Christian life is not easy. It's through sheer willpower, determination, and reliance on the Holy Spirit that we choose to follow our Savior through the race of life. We must choose to walk in His grace.

THE QUIGLEY

The Quigley is an intimidating 50-yard course in the muddy swamp behind Marine Officer Candidate School (OCS) in Quantico, Virginia. In 1976, 1st Lt William Quigley, OCS Tactics Officer, was tasked with creating the course to help Marines prepare for Vietnam. Thirty-three years later, they're still using it to make Marines.

It's mid-morning in the Quantico jungle. Already, the heat seems unbearable; the humidity, palpable. I sprint up the trail in woodland cammies with my M16A4 Service Rifle slung over my back, muzzle down, and my left hand gripping the barrel to keep it from jostling. Despite my best efforts to tighten the chinstrap, my Kevlar helmet now dances all over my head as I struggle up the trail to the edge of the Quigley, combat boots caked in mud. With my rifle butt, I manage to scrape some mud off as I catch my breath, intent on losing a few pounds before I jump in.

"Your turn, Candidate! Move!" the instructor yells in my ear. Holding my rifle overhead, I leap into the muddy water. I remember to bend my knees. Too many Marines have broken their legs over the years. I'm not getting sent home! It's deeper than I thought. I'm six foot six, and I'm soaked to my chest. I plunge forward, maneuvering into the sidestroke position and start swimming, quickly and quietly. My left hand gropes in front of me as my right hand holds the rifle just above the surface. I do this for about 25 yards. My right arm is dead. I can barely keep my weapon up.

Finally, I reach the first barrier. There are half-submerged telephone poles, four of them, about six feet apart, each spanning the length of the swampy channel. Razor wire stretches across the top of each.

"Put your rifle on top of the log!" I hear the instructor yell. "Feel under the log for mines or trip wire. Then, submerge underwater and up the other side. Do the same thing for all four!"

I'm just glad to rest the rifle on the log. I'm almost chuckling as it suddenly strikes me just how miserable all of this is. I take a deep breath and go under. Somehow, I manage to inhale a nose full of mud. I come up sputtering.

"Come on, Candidate!" I hear the instructor screaming. "This isn't drinking water! Now, move! Move!"

I snort out enough of that sewage to make a small mud pie and shove off to the next log. I'm more careful this time. I come up on the other side. Two more trips underwater and I make it past the last two logs, rifle still above the surface. I rub my eyelids with my free hand, trying to clear the mud. In front of me, I see a giant, cement culvert at least eight-feet long and submerged up to the brim.

"All right, College Boy!" the instructor yells. "You're going to lie on your back, rifle on your chest. Go underwater, headfirst through the pipe, using your feet to propel you."

I decided not to think about it. Seconds later, I'm on my back, rifle on top of me. I'm excruciatingly aware that my weapon is about to get very muddy. I take a huge breath and plunge under, moving head first through the pipe. My feet kick off the bottom, propelling me along. My Kevlar helmet bumps and scrapes against the ceiling. I think I'm almost through. Suddenly, my rifle almost gets ripped from my arms! The strap is caught on the bottom. Frantically, I'm groping at the strap, trying to free it. It's a big rock. I pull myself to it. I need air!

Desperately, I yank the strap free and lunge through the last of the pipe to the surface. I breech like a humpback whale and struggle to regain my footing as I gasp for breath. The instructor probably thinks I'm nuts. I don't care. I made it. I'm through! I swim the rest of the distance to the swamp's edge with what's now very likely a clogged rifle, and scramble up the bank.

On top, I clean debris from the M16's muzzle and sling it over my back again, muzzle down and with my left hand on the barrel. I cannot suppress a smile. Praise the Lord! I've conquered the Quigley! But this is far from over. I still have half the Combat Course to go. I let out a wild yell and take off down the trail.

CHRISTIAN LEADERSHIP WORLDVIEW – PRINCIPLE #12

The above anecdote was written by a United States Marine Officer and is overflowing with leadership principles and spiritual application. It is a compelling story written to inspire and motivate individuals to higher levels of personal achievement and discipline. This narrative is a "call to action" that embodies many of the Christian leadership characteristics needed to guide us in our journey here on earth.

While Christianity and godly living in this present world is a wonderful, spiritual blessing and honor, there are many trials and tribulations that we face and must work through each and every day. We are taught in the Bible to stay the course and be disciplined enough to run the race by the leading of the Holy Spirit. The Apostle Paul has much to say about "the race that is set before us." Here are just a few of the verses in the Bible:

"Wherefore seeing we also are compassed about with so great a cloud of witnesses, let us lay aside every weight, and the sin which doth so easily beset us, and let us run with patience the race that is set before us." (Hebrews 12:1)

"Know ye not that they which run in a race run all, but one receiveth the prize? So run, that ye may obtain." (1 Corinthians 9:24)

"I therefore so run, not as uncertainly; so fight I, not as one that beateth the air." (1 Corinthians 9:26)

"Holding forth the word of life; that I may rejoice in the day of Christ, that I have not run in vain, neither laboured in vain." (Philippians 2:16)

13

THE POWER OF TEAM

"Coming together is a beginning; keeping together is progress; working together is success."
Henry Ford

What a privilege it is to be an athlete in the United States of America in the twenty-first century. Many of today's athletes are accustomed to special treatment, notoriety, and financial remuneration that is beyond our wildest dreams and imaginations. Whether at a professional or an amateur level, if you are an athlete at the top of your game and considered world-class, by the world's standards, you are probably one of the "cool" people.

I must confess that I have a special place in my heart for athletes. It's not that I think athletes have any sort of super-spiritual connectivity to our Heavenly Father or that their God-given walk in life is any better or more important than the rest of ours. On the contrary, they also are wretched sinners that only can be saved by the grace of God. They are simply ordinary human beings that have been blessed with extraordinary gifts and talents from above. We see those gifts and talents on display on a regular basis. Many of us (Christians and non-Christians) are mesmerized and infatuated by what they are able to accomplish in their respective fields of athletic expertise. Athletics has become so engrained in our way of life and in today's popular culture that I would challenge anyone to try to avoid its influence and impact. Let's take a look at the power and influence of athletics by asking a few basic questions.

- Do you enjoy watching sporting events?
- How frequently do you and your children watch sporting events?

- When was the last time you saw an athlete interviewed on television?
- Can you name five well-known athletes?
- Do you regularly see articles on the internet or in print relating to the lives of well-known athletes?
- Are you or is someone you know interested in the life of a particular athlete?
- Have you ever seen an athlete on a billboard? In a commercial?
- Do you watch college football? How about the NFL? NBA? MLB? MLS?
- Do you or your children have a favorite athlete that you enjoy following?
- Is it considered quite a big deal when you see, talk with, or are around professional athletes?
- Does the world look up to and hold athletes to an almost god-like status?

Well, you get the idea. Athletics and athletes are everywhere. It is quite impossible to avoid their impact in the age we currently live in. Unfortunately, the world has branded today's athletes as larger-than-life figures that can do no wrong. They are idolized by children, teenagers, and adults around the globe. We follow their stories, watch their lives unfold in the national media, and incorporate their "goings-on" into our daily lives, interests, and routines. Many well-intentioned people look to athletes as role models and even believe they can provide moral and ethical guidance to help us make sense of the world. Others look to athletes and sports as mere diversions away from the complexities, pressures, and challenges of life that we routinely face. We are inspired by what they are able to accomplish on the field or court along with deep human interest and curiosity relating to their personal "back stories." By putting them on a pedestal, are we participating in the creation of these "superhuman" phenomes?

From a Christian perspective, is there anything good that can come from participating in sports and involving ourselves in the lives of athletes? That is the question that we want to consider in this chapter. What can we learn from the athletic realm that will help us shape a *Christian leadership worldview*?

First of all, I would like to share my own professional athletics story. I would like to give you a perspective of how athletics has helped to shape my Christian outlook and worldview. From a very early age, I have believed in the purity of sport and athletic competition. Even as an unsaved young man, it was never about fame and fortune. It always was about the drive and determination to be the best that I could be. I wanted to be able to hone the skills necessary to excel and to contribute to my teammates' success. There is no doubt that my teammates and I wanted to be winners.

As a result of all that drive and determination, I was able to play sports in high school, college, and then professionally. Yes, I was able to achieve a level of expertise in baseball that allowed me to get paid for playing a game. The Montreal Expos baseball team signed me to a professional baseball contract in June of 1983. I had just graduated from Brown University two weeks earlier. They put me on a plane to our spring training facility where I worked-out for a couple of weeks. Then, I was off to Calgary, Alberta, Canada, for my very first professional baseball season. That was where our "Class A" affiliate was located. I was in absolute shock and disbelief when I received that phone call from the Montreal Expos' general manager that summer day in June. Signing a professional baseball contract was a lifelong dream of mine that had finally come true! There were so many thoughts and questions that began whirling around in my head.

- What kind of teammates would I have?
- Would I be a starting player, or would I have to sit the bench for a while?
- Could I contribute?
- Did I have enough talent to get to the next level?

- Could I stay injury free?
- What other players did the Expos sign?
- What would the bus rides be like on the minor league circuit?
- What cities would we visit?
- Could I get to the major league one day?
- What would the hotels be like?
- Would I have enough money to pay for my room and meals?

As you can see, my focus as an unsaved 22-year old was not a spiritual one. It was primarily a self-centered worldview of the events of the day. Well, quite honestly, I probably didn't even know what the word "worldview" meant back then. I was a naïve country boy from the beautiful state of Maine who had average intelligence. The only difference between me and the guy next door was that I had a driving and insatiable competitive spirit. As a result, I had the propensity to out-work and out-hustle the competition. I made sure that I was the first person to arrive at the practice field and the last to leave. What I lacked in brains was made up in the gym, weight room, and the practice field. I just couldn't let it rest! I had to get better! I couldn't get enough of baseball and all that came with it.

Well, fortunately, there was a much better ending to my story than those of many other professional athletes. I got cut from the Montreal Expos' roster at the end of that 1983 season. I had a couple of major injuries that put me on the shelf and "out to pasture" for most of the season. A muscle tear in my shoulder and a major hamstring pull basically ended my dreams. Or did they? I know what you are thinking. That doesn't sound like much of a better ending to me!

God had a different plan for my life. He sent a teammate from Georgia to be a wonderful Christian witness and testimony for me during my one and only professional baseball season with the Expos. This young man was consistent in the way that he lived out his Christian faith, and that was attractive to me. We had long talks about Christ and the things that were missing in my life. Time and again, he told me that Christ was the answer and that I needed to change course and accept Him. He was a bold Christian witness.

After several months of conversation and the Holy Spirit working in my life, I decided to accept that free gift from God and become a follower of Jesus Christ in August of 1983. Very late one night after one of our games (11 p.m.), I decided to go out for a long jog. Guess where I ended up? Believe it or not, I ended up back on the Montreal Expos' minor league baseball field where we had just played a game a couple of hours before. Once I arrived at the field, I jumped the fence and ran out to centerfield. It was there that I got down on my knees and asked Christ to save me. I asked him to forgive me of my sins and to be my Lord and Savior. It was at that point in my life that I began to have a much deeper appreciation and clarity for the purity of sport.

There are so many Christian life-lessons and Bible applications to be learned from being involved in athletics. Because of my self-centered nature back then, I did not realize that, one day, God was going to use my baseball experiences and allow me to share my Christian testimony with others.

While the world primarily focuses on the fame, fortune, and celebrity of athletics, I would like us to consider the leadership dynamics of competition and sport. In other words, I want us to celebrate athletics from a personal growth perspective and for us to examine the purity of athletics. Let's take a look at a few of those building blocks of life.

- Leadership
- Victory
- Defeat
- Desire
- Discipline
- Regiment
- Integrity
- Honesty
- Performance

- Resilience
- Precision
- Support
- Recognition
- Teamwork

Yes, without question, athletics helped me to become a better leader. God allowed me to have the athletic experiences necessary to help me grow and prosper in the faith. Those experiences gave me the understanding, drive, and determination to want to share the gospel message of Christ around the world. Our family has much to be thankful for. We hope to make a positive impact on others for Christ.

One of the first lessons that great athletes have to learn is that there is no letter "I" in the words *team, teamwork,* or *teammate.* Great athletes and great teams understand that there needs to be chemistry and balance—*chemistry* in that everyone is fully utilizing their athletic gifts for the betterment of the team. Everyone has a role to play. Sound remotely familiar?

Don't we as followers of Jesus Christ use our spiritual gifts for the betterment of the Church? A fully-functioning church with optimal spiritual conditions is one where everyone is contributing and giving of themselves. God has blessed each of us with spiritual gifts that we should be using to help build the spiritual vibrancy that healthy local churches need.

Back to athletics. What about the balance that we talked about earlier? Great teams who exhibit maximum teamwork have a terrific balance of younger players mixed in with more experienced ones. Most of the championship teams I have played on or have had the pleasure of viewing on television have had this balance. They had a perfect blend of youth and experience for optimal conditions of performance.

We see this same phenomena within the local church framework. We have elders and senior saints with special gifts that complement the exuberance, idealism, and hubris of the young. God is able to move His work forward when there is a perfect blend of youth and experience. In a sense, it becomes a self-sustaining framework for local church growth, spiritual maturity, and worldwide Christian outreach.

Back to athletics. Beyond team chemistry and balance, there is one more binding force that drives great teams. You may have heard the expression, "I have my teammate's back." While this has become an overused and empty shell of a statement among many of today's athletes, if the onion is peeled back just a little, you will find much more depth and significance in the phrase than at first glance. What does the expression mean, and how does it apply in the athletic realm? Let's make several key observations about what the phrase, "I have my teammate's back", actually means.

1. **Contribute**: Your role and contribution is vital for the team to function at 100 percent capacity and beyond. In other words, your team needs you to contribute your athletic gifts to the best of your ability. Your contribution to the success of the team should not be linked to your role on the team. Whether you are the star scoring all of the points or the bench warmer cheering on his teammates, everyone has a part to play. The bottom line is that you must do your job and fulfill your role to the best of your abilities.
2. **Protect**: On and off the playing field, when your teammate is in trouble, you are going to be there to step up and pick them up. In a sense, you are going to protect their blind side. It may be a situation where you help minimize the impact of a busted play. As a teammate, it is your responsibility to anticipate and react to any advantage that the competition may have over one of your teammates. It is the same concept off the field. Your teammate needs you to help give guidance when he or she becomes misdirected.

3. **Evaluate:** You and your teammates are going to evaluate the playing conditions and course-correct when necessary. Through collaboration and teamwork, you are going to identify all of the necessary adjustments that need to be made in order to get the winning edge. Scour the landscape for potential adjustments on every play.
4. **Support:** You are going to support your teammates emotionally through the ups and downs of the game conditions. Encourage them when they are down, and give them the "high-fives" and an "atta boy" when they are knocking it out of the park.
5. **Team:** All of the praise and adulation is pointed to the team's success. There will be no self-aggrandizing commentary that points to self.

Well, I hope you now have a better understanding of what that phrase means to me as a former professional athlete. From a spiritual perspective, when I look into the Word of God, I see where the Lord has given to us examples of where He has protected us. To use a sports analogy, He has protected both our fronts and our backs. When the people of Israel were fleeing Egypt, God used a cloud by day and fire by night to provide light, direction, and comfort. He would never leave or forsake His people.

> "And the Lord went before them by day in a pillar of a cloud, to lead them the way; and by night in a pillar of fire, to give them light; to go by day and night: He took not away the pillar of the cloud by day, nor the pillar of fire by night, from before the people." (Exodus 13:21-22)

In the following few verses, we also see where God decided to move and protect their "rereward." The meaning of the word, "rereward", indicates that God would protect and guard them from behind. In other words, God had their backs.

> "And the angel of God, which went before the camp of Israel, removed and went behind them; and the pillar of the cloud went from before their face, *and stood behind them*: And it came between the camp of the Egyptians and the camp of Israel; and it was a cloud and darkness to them, but it gave light by night to these: so that the one came not near the other all the night." (Exodus 14:19-20)

> "For ye shall not go out with haste, nor go by flight: for the Lord will go before you; and the God of Israel will be your <u>rereward</u>." (Isaiah 52:12)

> "Is not this the fast that I have chosen? To loose the bands of wickedness, to undo the heavy burdens, and to let the oppressed go free, and that ye break every yoke? Is it not to deal thy bread to the hungry, and that thou bring the poor that are cast out to thy house? When thou seest the naked, that thou cover him; and that thou hide not thyself from thine own flesh? Then shall thy light break forth as the morning, and thine health shall spring forth speedily: and thy righteousness shall go before thee; the glory of the Lord shall be thy <u>rereward</u>. Then shalt thou call, and the Lord shall answer; thou shalt cry, and he shall say, Here I am. If thou take away from the midst of thee the yoke, the putting forth of the finger, and speaking vanity; And if thou draw out thy soul to the hungry, and satisfy the afflicted soul; then

shall thy light rise in obscurity, and thy darkness be as the noonday: And the Lord shall guide thee continually, and satisfy thy soul in drought, and make fat thy bones: and thou shalt be like a watered garden, and like a spring of water, whose waters fail not. And they that shall be of thee shall build the old waste places: thou shalt raise up the foundations of many generations; and thou shalt be called, The repairer of the breach, The restorer of paths to dwell in." (Isaiah 58:6-12)

Whether you are in ministry, business, nonprofit, athletics, or some other organizational environment, you have a responsibility to protect your teammate's back. There are many situations in life when the plays on your team unfold right before your eyes. Small adjustments are made here and there, but, in most cases, your teammates seem to be handling themselves as planned as the plays unfold. They are making all the right moves. But what happens when something goes wrong? How will you respond? Will you come to your teammates' rescue and fill the gap? Will you stand tall when times get tough? Will you have their backs?

I have come to believe that athletics is a wonderful training and proving ground for confronting the issues of life. It is especially valuable when born-again Christians can live out their faith in those competitive environments.

How are you doing as a teammate? Are you contributing, protecting, evaluating, supporting, and focused on team performance?

CHRISTIAN LEADERSHIP WORLDVIEW – PRINCIPLE #13

For the Christian, the value of athletics is not in fame, fortune, and notoriety. Athletics is a tool from above that helps us live out and "exercise" fundamental Christian beliefs. God has used athletics in my life for salvation purposes and to provide opportunities to proclaim the name of Christ. How will He use athletics in your life? Will you let Him?

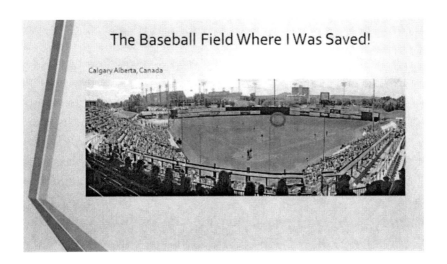

14

THE SERVANT LEADER

> *"You don't lead by hitting people over the head;*
> *that's assault, not leadership."*
> Dwight D. Eisenhower

Having had the pleasure of working in Corporate America for more than 30 years, I have been conditioned and trained to think about ways to get to the next level of performance. Much of this mindset can be attributed to the role that I played in Global Sales Strategy at my most recent place of employment. I also have been very fortunate to have worked for other outstanding organizations over the years in a strategist role. These organizations had strong performance-oriented cultures that made it easy to focus on increased productivity and better results. Every moment of every day at these businesses, we were trying to figure out how to innovate, motivate, positively disrupt, and exponentially impact the industries in which we were participating. We were trying endlessly to determine and uncover those seemingly insignificant nuggets lying just below the surface and beyond our grasp that could revolutionize our operations and make us better. In his book, *The Tipping Point*, Malcolm Gladwell goes into great depth on this subject.

In our executive meetings, we often contemplated things like coverage models, human relations approaches, go-to-market strategies, pricing strategies, distribution, product innovation, brand-building, and a host of other good business practices. All of these discussions are essential to business survival.

Then, we would move into the realm of teamwork, collaboration, and growing the next generation of leaders. These were developmental approaches of how and what our organization could do to move from "good to great" and beyond. These senior-management-level discussions are vital to the overall performance of any organization. Here are some examples of questions that were asked in these meetings:

- What does our succession planning look like?
- Who do we have in the leadership pipeline?
- What promotions and/or job rotations have they done?
- Have they had an assignment overseas?
- What do their performance reviews and results look like?
- Should we designate them as a leadership "fast track" type of employee?

As I have looked back over the years, I always have felt there was something missing in the approach. I couldn't put my finger on it, but I knew that there was that little something that we were not holding ourselves accountable for that could take us to the next level toward optimum performance.

Then, it struck me! We were "perfuming the pig" as it were to modify and project an image of leadership. We were focused on the strategies, tactics, and developmental issues that allowed us to check the boxes of all of those "experiential" elements of leadership without digging into the core of leadership itself. We worked hard at staying away from morality, core beliefs, and spiritual matters that make us who we are as leaders. We had never been willing to address the fundamental conditions of what makes great leaders, to talk about those things that impact the soul, or to enter into that "politically incorrect" space of building the soul components of leadership rather than building a façade of leadership.

How do we "build the soul" of effective leadership for tomorrow?

To be clear, I am not suggesting a list of do's and don'ts in a corporate policy handbook or sending someone away on a two-week trip to

New York City to get a better appreciation for the plight of the homeless. These are very worthy activities.

What I am talking about is a fundamental change in understanding who we are as human beings interacting in a social, corporate setting with employment responsibilities. We must understand that the real work of developing leaders lies at a much deeper level, a level that can train, condition, and mature a *Christian leadership worldview*.

Please do not misunderstand my point here. Gaining additional work experiences through various job rotations, getting plugged into the latest and greatest leadership training, working on an MBA, or even being assigned to a high-profile project all can help us build context and business acumen over the long term. But isn't that what every other great corporation in the world is doing? Are you really going to be any different than the 99.9 percent of other companies who focus on the same thing? How will you separate yourself from the rest of the pack?

SERVANT LEADERSHIP IS THE ANSWER

Corporations around the globe who want to get to the optimum level of performance must embrace a framework of servant leadership. Can you imagine what a corporate setting would look like in which there was a selfless focus on doing the right thing for God?

Here are a few questions to help us understand the heart of servant leadership...

- Could we be a better organization if we were focused more on others and their well-being than on ourselves and our career development?
- What if employees were promoted based primarily on their abilities to mentor, develop, and impact the lives of others?
- What would happen if any type of behavior that was self-promoting and/or self-aggrandizing was immediately "called out" and left at the door?

- What if our decision-making process was void of pride and concern for who gets credit for what but rather was a sincere collaboration in pursuit of what is in the best interests of the organization? What type of tone would that set for your company?
- What if a hiring process was put in place that attracted servant leaders? Do you think that, over time, your corporate culture would change for the good?
- How about the things we use to measure success? What if we started measuring performance indicators primarily related to servant leadership and people development?
- What would happen if our mission and vision statements clearly articulated a performance culture dominated by servant leadership?
- What would your organization look like if the mean-spiritedness, win-at-all-costs mentalities, and "I-am-the-smartest-guy-in-the-room" attitudes were removed from your meetings and boardrooms?
- Can you imagine with me for a moment a situation where the corporate boardroom was full of executives who were humble to the core?

I believe that many in the corporate world today greatly misunderstand this phenomenon called servant leadership. They believe the phrase is synonymous with weakness. Some do not believe in the concept of servant leadership. Others believe that it would take too much time to change the corporate culture.

The fact is that you can be both hard-charging and a servant leader at the same time. When you identify the character traits of someone that is hard-charging (e.g. enthusiastic personality, commitment, and dedication to a cause, etc.) you realize that these are not isolated traits separate from what makes a great leader. They are, in fact, complimentary to what makes a great leader!

The fault lies in a focus and end goal that is intrinsically self-serving. Great leadership cries for the correct focus and balance to have both traits in equal measure. What good is a servant leader who doesn't stand up and lead? And what good is a hard-charger who doesn't practice servant leadership?

This brings me back to what corporations must do within their organizations to achieve optimum performance. They need to work on their employees' spiritual development. They need to dig in and believe that the Bible has all of the answers to leadership. They need to embrace a management philosophy in which "building the soul" of their employees is the only clear path to optimum performance. Taking that issue on will require some grit, determination, and intestinal fortitude from key senior leadership positions.

> "And the things that thou hast heard of me among many witnesses, the same commit thou to faithful men, who shall be able to teach others also."
> (2 Timothy 2:2)

> "He riseth from supper, and laid aside his garments; and took a towel, and girded himself. After that he poureth water into a basin, and began to wash the disciples' feet, and to wipe them with the towel wherewith he was girded." (John 13:4-5)

> "Let another man praise thee, and not thine own mouth; a stranger, and not thine own lips."
> (Proverbs 27:2)

> "Put not forth thyself in the presence of the king, and stand not in the place of great men: For better it is that it be said unto thee, Come up hither; than that thou shouldest be put lower in the presence of the prince whom thine eyes have seen."
> (Proverbs 25:6-7)

> "And thou say in thine heart, My power and the might of mine hand hath gotten me this wealth."
> (Deuteronomy 8:17)

> "But thou didst trust in thine own beauty, and playedst the harlot because of thy renown, and pouredst out thy fornications on everyone that passed by; his it was." (Ezekiel 16:15)

Finally, lest anyone in the corporate world think that I have totally lost my mind about flipping the primary focus area to what some would call the *softer* leadership issue of spiritual development, we must stay equally engaged in overall organizational performance. Yes, we need a balance. We need to be both hard-charging toward key financial metrics while leading change in the human development front.

CHRISTIAN LEADERSHIP WORLDVIEW – PRINCIPLE #14

Those organizations that are able to build and broaden the spiritual development and core leadership characteristics of their employees will be industry frontrunners. Because of the politically-correct environment that companies must operate and navigate within today, most tend to shy away from taking the spiritual element on. Yet encouraging employees to get involved in church and learning about servant leadership is a wonderful thing!

15

ORGANIZATIONAL DECISION-MAKING

"Repetition of the same thought or physical action develops into a habit which, repeated frequently enough, becomes an automatic reflex."
Norman Vincent Peale

Let's examine for a moment a Christian leader's decision-making process and the need for collaboration, consultation, and the employment of wise counsel. While we are all well aware that those at the tops of organizational heirarchies are ultimately responsible for results, and the proverbial "the-buck-stops-here" mantra is in full force, there is a myriad of other potential influencers who help shape the process.

The same is true for the leaders of a family unit. We desperately need to seek the counsel of others before making critical decisions. The Word of God reinforces this approach with numerous verses. For example, the Bible has approximately 182 instances where the word, "counsel", is used. There is an expectation from above that we will avail ourselves to wise counsel before making major decisions. Any time you can bounce various ideas, thoughts, and potential strategies off trusted, godly advisors, the better off you will be. Seeking the input and counsel of others is a five-tier process.

1. A leader must provide followers with an environment to offer their thoughts and insights without fear of retribution. It is the leader's responsibility to create the "safe havens" and the culture for their followers to be free to contribute. Tier #1 is all about being creative and coming up

with as many different approaches and solutions as possible. Here, you simply brainstorm with your team to think through all of the relevant issues. Let your team's creative juices flow!

2. You start to categorize the various ideas for those with common themes. In Tier #2, you start to refine, clarify, and prioritize the most important elements. With your guidance, your followers and immediate team members are quite capable of assisting you in narrowing down the priority list.

3. Once you have narrowed down those broader themes into category headers, then you move on to Tier #3. This is where you start to bring in other important key stakeholders in order to build consensus. These stakeholders have enough political clout and influence to be needed in the decision-making process. If not, they are very capable of becoming "blockers" to a go-forward decision. Ultimately, you are trying to find common ground and get support to move your initiative forward. Remember, in each tier of the decision-making process, you are refining and crafting the optimal conditions.

4. Then, you seek third-party counsel or others that may provide additional subject matter expertise. In Tier #4, you may even go outside of your immediate organization to engage others to get a completely different perspective. Benchmarking and evaluating the processes of other individuals and organizations can help you put things in perspective. Often times, benchmarking will allow you to go down entirely different rabbit trails for comparison purposes. This step will help you to

further analyze and synthesize the major components of your decision.
5. In Tier #5, this is where the leader needs to pull the trigger. Through much prayer and godly counsel, a decision must be made. A leader must be decisive in their final determination. With all of the involvement and input from their followers, the wise counsel of their peers, and the clarity received from our Lord, a decision must be made. You must believe expectantly that your decision is the right one.

At this point, your work has just begun. You now have a responsibility to make sure that the final decisions are communicated back down through the organization. As a leader, you should set the communication tempo and messaging. You must make sure that the messages that are cascading down through the organization are the right ones and those that you intended. A report back from those delivering the message and a feedback loop from those hearing the message must be required.

The same is true in the family unit. When decisions are made, they need to be communicated back down to all of the family members for clarity. The best decisions that are poorly communicated can ultimately fall apart.

What does the Bible say about *counsel*?

> "Behold, ye are all children of Israel; give here your advice and counsel." (Judges 20:7)

> "Without counsel purposes are disappointed: but in the multitude of counsellors they are established." (Proverbs 15:22)

"Hear counsel, and receive instruction, that thou mayest be wise in thy latter end." (Proverbs 19:20)
"Every purpose is established by counsel: and with good advice make war." (Proverbs 20:18)

"We took sweet counsel together, and walked unto the house of God in company." (Psalms 55:14)

CHRISTIAN LEADERSHIP WORLDVIEW – PRINCIPLE #15

Working our way through the many important decisions of organizational life can be taxing for Christians. How can we really know that we are making the right decisions? The first step is to make sure you are filtering everything through His Word. Next, spend an enormous amount of time in prayer. Lastly, make sure you involve others in the process and use them as sounding boards. They should be reliable and trustworthy individuals. Christians should have a clear process of thinking for making organizational, personal, and family-related decisions.

16

FILTERING ORGANIZATIONAL NOISE

> *"I believe in Christianity as I believe that the sun has risen:
> not only because I see it, but because by it I see everything else."*
> *C. S. Lewis*

Organizational leaders, student leaders, athletes, and our church leaders of today must allow the Bible to be both the "filter" and the "potter" in shaping their *Christian leadership worldviews*. Romans 12:2 is very clear on the issue:

> "And be not conformed to this world: but be ye transformed by the renewing of your mind, that ye may prove what is that good, and acceptable, and perfect, will of God."

As leaders, God has placed us in positions where we influence others by taking action. Therefore, we must be so closely in synch and aligned to the Word of God that our every thought, conversation, motivation, and action is dominated by the leading of the Holy Spirit. As leaders, we are obligated to have a God-consciousness that is so disciplined that everything is filtered through the Bible.

Remember, the world is watching closely. They want to see how you handle yourself when you are under pressure. They are evaluating what you say and how you say it. They will take note of all of your earthly mistakes. Allow the cross of Calvary and the blood of Christ to permeate the leader in you!

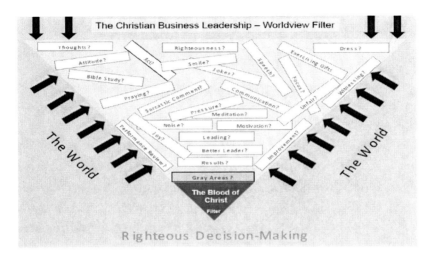

CHRISTIAN LEADERSHIP WORLDVIEW – PRINCIPLE #16

Has there ever been a better roadmap for life than the Word of God? Just think about it for one second. The Bible is a verbally-inspired, God-breathed, inerrant, infallible, and perfect book written by 40 ordinary men who were led by the Holy Spirit! Wow!

17

Developing Policy: A Homeschool Primer

> *"I am afraid that the schools will prove the very gates of hell, unless they diligently labor in explaining the Holy Scriptures and engraving them in the heart of the youth."*
> *Martin Luther*

Pastors and Christian school administrators across our great country need to discuss, analyze, debate, and pray about a growing dilemma in the Church body as it relates to Christian education. There has been an explosion among church members who have elected to home school their children, which has created a host of new and challenging issues for Christian school educators. Many local churches, their Christian schools, and the corresponding school boards do not know how to respond or react to this widespread choice of teaching children in the home. Some local church bodies are trying to address the issues while others are ignoring the home-school phenomena. A small group of churches even are taking a staunch, anti-home-schooling position.

Whatever your position currently is, I hope that this chapter will heighten your awareness about the thoughts and feelings about the home school family and will bring churches and Christian schools alike to the understanding that they must formulate and communicate a coherent policy on this issue.

Why home school? Philosophically, this is a question that elicits a host of responses depending upon the Christian parents to whom you are talking. Some parents are home school zealots who believe that this is the only "right way" to teach their children and protect them from the pressures and sins of the world's system. Other parents simply feel that the Lord has given to them the ability, patience, and call to be able to teach their children in the home and want to follow the Lord's leading in this matter. Some parents are deathly afraid of the effects that a public school (we will call this "government school" hereafter) would have on their children. Others still can't afford to send their children anywhere else and want to avoid the government schools.

Theologically, however, there is one common theme that all Christian parents would give as the primary reason to teach their children in the home. They all want to see their children taught Biblical principles and raised in the "nurture and admonition of the Lord" (Ephesians 6:4). Home-school parents desire for their children to become more Christ-like. As members of Bible-believing churches, a home-school parent's desires are no different than families who elect to send their children to Christian schools which exist as a ministry to those same Bible-believing churches.

Let us take a look at a fictional church that could be representative of the constitution and by-laws of many churches and Christian schools across America. The Christian school states,

1. The Christian Academy exists as a ministry of the Baptist Church in order that the Christian parents may be assisted in their God-given responsibility to bring their children up "in the nurture and admonition of the Lord" (Ephesians 6:4). Recognizing that all truth is God's, the Bible is upheld as the unifying basis of all the academic disciplines and the guide to all interpretation of reality.
2. Desiring to see each student strive for Christ-likeness, the Baptist Christian Academy seeks to train Christian youth of every ability in the highest principles of Christian leadership, self-discipline, individual responsibility, personal integrity, and good citizenship.

3. The board of deacons of the Baptist Church serves as the school board of the Baptist Christian Academy. To expedite school business matters, a school committee including pastors, principal, three deacons, and various parents of academy students meet regularly.

I praise the Lord for this one fictitious church's clear vision of what the purpose and responsibility of the Christian Academy really is. As it states, it exists as a ministry to assist Christian parents. It would appear that home-school parents and Christian-school parents would be in total agreement and alignment as it relates to their children, or are they?

So what are those new and challenging issues facing our pastors and Christian school administrators across our country as it relates to Christian education?

There is a growing number of home-school families who want to access part of the Christian school ministry, whether it be academically, athletically, or both. This particular group of home-school parents feel they can broaden the scope of their children's education by having the Christian school *assist* in specific areas of academic or athletic training and discipline. They feel that—as part of the local body of believers who support the church (of which the Christian school is a ministry) with their time, tithes, prayers, and dedication—their children's educational needs should be addressed. These parents feel that the Lord has given to them one opportunity to teach their children and prefer not to send them to a government school or alternative Christian academy to seek that additional academic or athletic training. They desire to get that additional training within the context of their own local body of believers. They understand that, legally, they are entitled to access those aspects of the government school they feel would enhance the development of their children. However, they do not desire to unite with any part of the government school system.

There are many churches today who have decided not to allow integration of their home-school family members into the Christian schools. In the past, the position has been all or nothing. This simply means that you either enroll your children into the Christian school or you elect to go the home-school or the government-school route. There has been little to no room for the home-school parents to maneuver and access part(s) of the Christian school ministry.

Parents want choices. Parents would like to design and craft educational experiences that are unique and specific for the individual child based on their particular aptitudes and interests. This situation has created a unique dilemma and is very perplexing at its core.

In many instances across our beautiful country, the local church body willingly and strategically gives financial support to their Christian school ministries. These Christian schools are working with very tight budgets and need financial support from their local church. This has created situations from the pulpit where family members are asked to financially support (by faith) the Christian school ministries but are denied access to various parts of that same ministry! Praise the Lord that we have a great God who can work out all of the minor details of Christian education!

The Bible-believing churches today who have decided not to integrate the home-school families have an additional challenge ahead of them of keeping the unity and harmony among the brethren. We must not let this become a divisive issue in the Church body. The ability to keep this unity will be one of the biggest challenges that a pastor will face in the future. While disagreement about non-integration of home-school families may not manifest itself in outright rebellion or resentment, there will be an "understanding" that participation and access has been denied. There always will be a question and notes of concern from the homeschool contingent? Does the local church really care about the godly development of my children? While I know in my heart that they do and the answer is yes, the decision to stay the course of non-integration leaves lingering questions and points to a less- compassionate point of view. This is an especially difficult decision because, in the flesh, you are talking about denying a parent's child the opportunity for growth while it is certainly within the local church's decision-making authority and purview to grant that access. This can be a highly-charged emotional issue when you are talking about a child's godly development. Meanwhile, the government schools across America would welcome them with open arms.

Total unity and harmony will not be realized among the brethren until the local church leaders have communicated a clear position on this issue and have correspondingly formulated a cohesive policy. We need to get on our knees before our God and ask for His wisdom and direction in this matter.

I truly believe that a day is coming when pastors will stand up behind the pulpit, take their notes out of their Bible, glance up at their congregation as they get ready to preach, and realize a very curious thing. They will realize that a very large part of their local church body has decided to homeschool their children. That pastor suddenly will realize what his vision is for the future concerning Christian education.

I envision a local body of believers rejoicing that the Christian school ministry is a ministry for the entire church body. It is a ministry open to all church members in good standing to be able to teach their children God-honoring principles. I envision a local body of believers where total integration has taken place. All church members will have a genuine love for one another's children while participating in their development and guidance.

I envision a local body of believers where church members have access to all or parts of the ministries of the local church body, a local body where all of the members are excited about supporting the Christian school ministry with their time, money, and prayers. They will be excited about supporting the Christian school because the school is totally integrated. It will be considered a ministry because all members have access.

I envision a Christian school where the focus is on loving, developing, and teaching one another's children without worrying about who gets the praise or recognition. It will be a body of believers where there is total harmony and agreement about the function of Christian education, not one where there is any degree of separation or exclusivity. It will be one where godly principles of Christian discipline are enforced for both Christian school and homeschool children alike… where the standards are firm, fair, and God-honoring.

It will be a local body where there is one goal, one purpose, and one vision! Praise the Lord!

> "Behold, how good and how pleasant it is for brethren to dwell together in unity!" (Psalm 133:1)

> "Endeavoring to keep the unity of the Spirit in the bond of peace." (Ephesians 4:3)

> "And, ye fathers, provoke not your children to wrath: but bring them up in the nurture and admonition of the Lord." (Ephesians 6:4)

CHRISTIAN LEADERSHIP WORLDVIEW – PRINCIPLE #17

What a blessing it is to be able to teach our children in the home. Likewise, it is an equal blessing to be able to send our children to a Christian school. And yes, there are some Christians who would argue that the public school system is best for their children. To a parent, there is nothing more important than the development of a child. As Christians, we should encourage and pray for one another concerning the upbringing of our children. The education of our children should not be a divisive issue at all. It should bring us together in a spirit of unity.

18

WHAT IS YOUR COMMUNICATION STRATEGY?

"I have talked with great men, and I do not see how they differ from others."
Abraham Lincoln

As Christian leaders, we have the gift of God's written and inspired Word to help cleanse, guide, teach, mold, and inspire us to unimagined spiritual insight and understanding. It is only through the power of His Word that these things can be accomplished. There is nothing that we can add to our Christian journey outside of the grace of God that will exponentially impact or fundamentally change God's plan and design for life here on this earth.

While God has given man a free will, His will ultimately will be accomplished in our lives. Our human intellect, ingenuity, and creative genius (so we think) pales in comparison to the wisdom of our Alpha and Omega, the Creator God. We simply serve at the pleasure of our Lord and Savior, Jesus Christ, through our obedience. As we grow and yield to His calling in our lives, we do so not out of any selfish or fleshly motivation but out of a heart that is willing to praise the Name of our Lord.

If we truly believe that the statements above are true and that God is sovereign and in full and complete control, why then do we feel it necessary to help Him along the way? Why do we feel it necessary to add those extra-biblical and man-made arguments about issues that do nothing to edify the brethren or further the cause of Christ? Many times, these arguments turn into prideful, intellectual, and dogmatic pursuits and debates that have no place in Christian learning, growth, or edification.

In this chapter, I will argue that even the most gifted and fortunate among us must communicate and "keep it simple" for maximum Christian impact. Knowledge can be a very dangerous thing when it is used to feed the flesh. Quite frankly, many human beings (Christians, pastors, and myself included) have a natural propensity (the old man) toward self-aggrandizement and the "look-what-I-have-accomplished" style of leadership that needs to be called out, modified, and amended. Those among us with this predisposition operate with a strong sense of self and ego-drive that strive for ongoing acclamation and praise. These individuals often will land in doctrinal rabbit trails in order to satisfy those intellectual desires and pursuits. Intellectuals can fill volumes with extra-Biblical arguments and things that the Bible does not make clearly evident. These narratives and man-made arguments on the surface seem to make a whole lot of sense! They have a logical basis of thought, tell a nice story, and are flawlessly delivered. Unfortunately, there is no substance or depth, and the arguments are not sourced in absolute truth. They are simply opinions on subjects that cannot be supported by the Word of God. The Word of God warns us again and again about intellectualism in its most wretched and earthly form.

> "Beware lest any man spoil you through philosophy and vain deceit, after the tradition of men, after the rudiments of the world, and not after Christ."
> (Colossians 2:8)

It is very clear from this verse in Colossians that we are to seek the message of Christ rather than traditional and man-made thoughts steeped in humanism. In this present day and age, it is very easy for Christians to become lulled to sleep (and entertained for that matter) by intellectual thought and diversions that have nothing to do with the Bible. Yet, they are convinced their reasoning has Biblical origins.

> "Of these things put them in remembrance, charging them before the Lord that they strive not about

words to no profit, but to the subverting of the hearers." (2 Timothy 2:14)

God is telling us in *2 Timothy* that we should be focused on the critical doctrines in His Word and not arguing and debating about some individual words that have no spiritual value. He is reminding us that this type of discussion could undermine the authority of the Bible and the intent of specific passages. We must keep a holistic perspective and understand the entirety of the Bible by comparing scripture with other portions of scripture. When we strive about words, often times, we do so in order to "win" the conversation and further our own points of view on issues that are not directly relevant.

"Be of the same mind one to another. Mind not high things, but condescend to men of low estate. Be not wise in your own conceits." (Romans 12:16)

In *Romans*, God reminds us that we need to relate to one another on even and similar plains. As one man put it long ago, "We are not to be so high and heavenly-minded that we are no earthly good." In other words, we need to be able to relate to people on their level. We are not to put on "airs" along with any false modesty or pretense. Instead, we are instructed to be real and genuine when we minister and relate to one another. We are not to be so caught up with peripheral and high-minded issues that our opinion of ourselves is much more than would adequately represent our current state… that being filthy, wretched sinners saved by the grace of God.

"Ever learning, and never able to come to the knowledge of the truth." (2 Timothy 3:7)

God points out that knowledge for the sake of knowledge is meaningless. Outside of the truth contained in His Word, it is nothing more than an intellectual exercise full of vanity. Enormous amounts of time and money can be spent learning useless and anecdotal bits of information that will not glorify our Savior. The Bible tells us that this form of learning is ongoing and will never lead us to our desired ends.

> "They are corrupt, and speak wickedly concerning oppression: they speak loftily." (Psalm 73:8)

God examines the folly of wicked and foolish men. Not only do they speak wickedly, but they use high-minded, intellectual, and lofty reasoning to support their wicked and evil ways.

> "For our rejoicing is this, the testimony of our conscience, that *in simplicity and godly sincerity*, not in fleshly wisdom, but by the grace of God, we have had our conversation in the world, and more abundantly to you-ward." (2 Corinthians 1:12)

Here, God rebuffs intellectualism in favor of simplicity and godly sincerity. He is not interested in the thoughts and opinions of this world. Rather, He wants us to focus on and engage in spiritual conversations by the grace of God that will make an impact on fellow believers, conversations based on the wisdom of God and not the fleshly wisdom of man.

It reminds me of one of the early and great missionaries from North America to the country of Burma (now Myanmar). Adoniram Judson was held up in the world's eyes as a figure that was larger than life. As a missionary, he endured many trials and hardships for the cause of Christ. Yet, when he came back to America on furlough after more than 40 years on the mission field, all he wanted to do was talk about the simple message of salvation based on the shed blood of Jesus Christ. For him, it was the simplicity of the gospel message that meant more to him than anything. Adoniram's message and communication was not about him or his accomplishments but squarely was focused on the Savior.

On the other hand, studying the deep and profound truths of God's Word can have immediate and lasting impact in our lives and can be extremely beneficial in our testimony to others. God encourages us to diligently study His Word and move from the milk of his word to strong meat. He expects us to rightly divide the Word of Truth.

> "As newborn babes, desire the sincere milk of the word, that ye may grow thereby." (1 Peter 2:2)

God tells us that we should have a thirst for the knowledge of spiritual things in His Word so that we can grow. However, as we have learned previously, it is not the kind of growth we get from high and lofty thinking but from the sincere milk of the Word of God. It is growth that comes from the simplicity and sincerity of the gospel message of Christ.

> "Study to show thyself approved unto God, a workman that needeth not to be ashamed, rightly dividing the word of truth." (2 Timothy 2:15)

We are to be workmen by studying the doctrinal issues that will be pleasing to God. We are to do this in an approach to His Word that is orderly and consistent with the whole counsel of God. Only then can we move to a point in life where we can lead and teach others.

Some would argue that this approach doesn't sound like a whole lot of fun. They would ask, "Are you saying the Bible can be the only source of enjoyment and inspiration?" If so, they would be missing the entire point of this chapter. There are many other intellectual pursuits outside of scripture that bring us enjoyment. For example, history, literature, mathematics, and other academic areas are full of opportunities to broaden our thinking. However, if we are searching for the true meaning of life, it is the Word of God that will give us the answers and show us the way to salvation. If we get so caught up and consumed with those other areas of interest, allowing the important things of the Lord to disappear, our focus then becomes misguided.

Let us summarize the main points of this chapter.

- Outside of the instruction in God's Word, the intellectual pursuits of meaningless facts, figures, philosophies, and man-made wisdom after the tradition of men is vanity and useless for spiritual growth.
- God encourages us to diligently and rigorously explore the learning, instruction, and counsel found in His Word.
- As Christian leaders in the army of God, we should learn to simplify the messaging to fellow believers in ways that are clearly relatable to others. Christ was our example here. He used parables to simplify deep, spiritual concepts into bits of information that we could understand. No matter how gifted one may be or what educational level one may have obtained, Christians should learn to "keep it simple" for the edification of fellow believers and the furtherance of the kingdom of God. We must learn to wade through and understand the issues of complexity, synthesize and simplify key concepts, and then be able to relate and teach them to others with a child-like simplicity. We do this in a Christ-like manner. Praise God!
- Lastly, we can and should enjoy outside interests as long as they do not become obsessions and the only focal points in our lives.

> **CHRISTIAN LEADERSHIP WORLDVIEW – PRINCIPLE #18**
>
> If you want to make an impact on the masses with the truth of God's Word, the ability to simplify the messaging is paramount to success. Intellectual diatribes have no place in our local churches. The simple message of the gospel is sweet music to the hearers. Don't be impressed with man's wisdom. If what is being communicated from the pulpit does not match up with the Bible, be quick to confront the communication to gain a fuller understanding of what is being taught.

19

ROARING THUNDER

"Money has never made man happy, nor will it. There is nothing in its nature to produce happiness. The more of it one has, the more one wants."
Benjamin Franklin

You gathered together the waters
and saw that it was good,
the glistening perfection of the deep
divided with such peace and tranquility.

Yet those rambunctious little darling waves
so determined and full of boundless energy,
pressing forward again and again and again
to conquer, to strive, to win… let us run.

Curling upward with a symphonic thrust,
frolicking, dancing together they mount high,
a focus and determination like no other,
so much splendor, the infinite challenge to express.

"How far can we reach?" they muse.
"How high will we crest?" they consider.
"Will we crash with awesome power?" they contemplate.
"Will we score the coastline of success?" they wonder.

An indelible mark, a legacy to provide,
bigger and better, yes, more to get.
Our forefathers understand our plight.
They paved our paths straight ahead.

"For posterity, the children!" they exclaimed.
The highest, the longest, the *roaring thunder*
look at me with awesome power to possess
to travel further with a majestic view of self.

A better curl, an inspiring mount,
another turn we must now take.
Our little waves do recede for us to run again.
If we fall short… our pride says. No… We must.

"But wait. The human race do we view.
The American Dream… it is ours," they boast.
"The dwelling, the auto, and mammon, too.
We strive with unwavering zeal."

"To live our lives in want of gathering
happiness. Just around the corner,
one more thing to fulfill our heart's desire.
We connive. We plan to manipulate our ends."

"The future is ours to get to be fully satisfied.
One more mount, ambition near,
the dreams and hopes of the material.
But where is Christ Jesus in all of this?"

Remember the Lord. He is your center.
He is the splendor of your American Dream,
the prize to score Christ's nature on human-kind,
boasting of Him with the *roaring thunder* of His Word.

Such a place as this, your expansive ocean blue,
the calming holy nature, let us take rest,
Serenity and peace to sooth the mind and soul.
Your creation, may it teach us the many lessons of life.

CHRISTIAN LEADERSHIP WORLDVIEW – PRINCIPLE #19

This poem was written as an allegory to depict an unhealthy focus on the material things of this world, a focus that exponentially takes us away from things above. It starts us out with the purity of a God who created the ocean blue with all of its beauty and splendor and has a true appreciation for His creation. We watch the waves rise and fall as they pound the coastlines of our country again and again. A continuous onslaught of desire, power, and determination is evident with these crashing and magnificent waves.

The poem then relates the narrative back to the human race and how we strive for the material things of this world. We strive for the "American Dream" not unlike the endless quest of the ocean waves crashing the coastline except our determination and zeal become an obsession with power, prestige, and fame. We negligently run the race of a lifetime only to find our spiritual center has drifted off into oblivion.

Lastly, the poem challenges us to return to our Savior and to keep our eyes upon Him.

Don't let the material things of this world distract you from the important issues of life. Faith and family are the true riches of life.

20
CHURCH STRATEGY IN THE 21ST CENTURY

"We have learned to live with unholiness and have come to look upon it as the natural and expected thing."
Aiden Wilson Tozer

This chapter was written with a sense of love, passion, and concern for the well-being of God's Church. There are tactics and strategies being used by many church leaders around the world to reach the masses that I consider to be dangerous and detrimental to the long-term and sustainable growth of local, New Testament churches. Having a dissenting opinion on the particular tactics being used for church growth is not very popular among today's church leaders.

Many Christians who are devoted to the faith mistakenly have gone down a path that I believe will hurt the cause of Christ. Only time will tell the full impact of their decision making. While I point out and make blunt statements that run counter to their current direction and beliefs, it is with a heavy heart that I must make these claims.

Over the years, there have been other messages that have not fit the popular sentiments of the day. While the discussion below will in no way be equivalent to the importance or eloquence of those previous warnings just mentioned, I hope that it will encourage a healthy debate and cause people within the church to think about charting our way forward toward a healthier *Christian leadership worldview.*

For example, Jonathan Edwards preached a compelling sermon called, "Sinners in the Hands of an Angry God." This message sparked the beginning of one of the most significant spiritual awakenings that our country has ever known.

Another well-known evangelist and theologian of that period, Gilbert Tennent, wrote a stirring and equally controversial sermon titled, "On the Danger of an Unconverted Ministry." This too cut to the bone of the Presbyterian clergy and sparked a much-needed discussion on the issue of salvation in the ranks of senior church leaders.

As a comparison, let us now contemplate some of the strategies that many of the major big-box retailers use to achieve their relative greatness in the world of business.

1. **Logistics**: Most big-box retailers have advanced supply chain and distribution networks around the globe.
2. **Product Variety**: It is "soup to nuts." For the most part, there is very little that you will not be able to purchase at these stores if you are a consumer.
3. **E.D.L.P.**: This is one of the "hooks" in my opinion. Generally speaking, shoppers know that many big-box retailer's products will be priced lower than or equal to the competition. Yes, there may be items here or there that are priced a little higher, but their corporate mantra and marketing focus is to provide "Everyday Low Prices." At the very least, these stores have done a nice job of creating this perception.
4. **Reasonable Quality**: While the product quality may not be in the Louis Vuitton range, they do hold their suppliers to a reasonable level of quality. They provide at least enough quality to keep their consumers from revolting and leaving for the competition.
5. **Location, Location, Location**: The big-box retailers do in-depth studies to find the locations that will draw the biggest crowds. They want to be

where the action is in order to maximize per-store revenues.
6. **Technology**: Most have become leaders in the use of technology. Their route optimization software along with their TMS (Transportation Management Systems) and WMS (Warehouse Management Systems) are some of the best in the world.

In a nutshell, these big-box retailers are the masters of leveraging their suppliers, running an efficient operation, and using technology to the fullest extent while providing cheap and semi-reliable products that can be accessed in convenient locations.

So what does this have to do with Christianity and the Church?

There has been a movement over the past few decades toward what I will call a "Christian consumerism" approach to worship. There is a very strange and eerie parallel to what is happening with the local body of believers. The Church as a whole has adopted a retail mentality. In this chapter, I will provide several examples of how the big-box retail stores and the "super churches" of today have much in common.

First, I will compare the **"everyday-low-price"** approach of most big-box stores with the super churches' ability to draw in the masses with a cheaper version of the gospel. The Bible and its impact have been so watered down that the Word of God has been relegated to nothing more than a mantel piece. The Word of God is referred to occasionally in the abstract but only when it fits a social gospel and all-inclusive mentality. Yes, this is the hook. Give them just enough (a cheapened version) to draw them in and keep them entertained to fill the coffers. These super churches work hard not to step on anyone's toes, for they want everyone to feel comfortable and enjoy the "event" experience. The church goers like it because they do not have to invest as much emotional or spiritual capital into their Sunday mornings. Congregations can hang around the fringes without making any real commitment to change.

"That we henceforth be no more children, tossed to and fro, and carried about with every wind of doctrine, by the sleight of men, and cunning craftiness, whereby they lie in wait to deceive." (Ephesians 4:14)

Second, let us compare the **product variety** and the breadth and depth of all the "stuff" you can buy at the big-box stores for relatively cheap and fair prices. Isn't that part of the allure when you shop in these types of stores? There is a fairly good chance that they will have what you want or at least a close substitute.

Ditto for the megachurches of today. They want to tickle the ears of everyone who walks through their doors. They want to create an experience that is satisfying to everyone in the broadest sense of the term. Retailers and the super-churches of today want to make sure that they keep you coming back through the doors and spending/giving more money. They will only be able to keep you coming back if they appeal to the broadest spectrum of "Christian consumers" as possible.

How do you do that? You take customer survey after customer survey, study the dominant buying needs of the consumer, look at purchase activity, and provide solutions and products that meet their individual needs. In the case of the church, it is no longer about preaching the whole truth of the gospel and sounding out the message of absolute truth. It is about putting on a demonstration, event, and/or performance that reaches the masses. You simply find out what the church members want and give it to them.

You see this experience playing out with the multiple sermons being preached at many of the megachurches of today. One service is put on for those who like contemporary "events" while another is put on for the more traditional approach to worship. In other words, the importance of absolute truth, unity, and that horizontal covenant relationship with fellow believers only applies based upon the needs and the wants of the church members themselves! Basically, they are indicating that the authority of the Bible is secondary to the wants and needs of their congregations.

Does this seem a little backwards to anyone? How disappointing is this? Are we to let human desires, human satisfaction, and entertainment trump the purity and holiness of God's Word?

> "Beware lest any man spoil you through philosophy and vain deceit, after the tradition of men, after the rudiments of the world, and not after Christ." (Colossians 2:8)

Third is the issue of the **quality of the product offerings**. Like most major retailers, the super-churches work hard at providing the ultimate church experience. You have heard me say this before, and I think it is worth repeating. If churches have a "come-as-you-are-and-go-as-you-were" mentality, there will be very little evidence of spiritual growth. They can put on event performances that would even have the big-box stores wringing their hands with envy. They could draw in the masses with good-quality performances, continue to give them what they want, and then pass the offering hat around. For now, it seems like a fairly successful business model.

> "Having a form of godliness, but denying the power thereof: from such turn away." (2 Timothy 3:5)

Fourth, what about the **technology**? Boy, do the super-churches ever have technology. They have three or four screens with state-of-the-art video technology. They have the most sophisticated electric guitars that will rock your brain, literally. Because they are currently appealing to a much younger audience, there is no lack of technological skill and savvy. These folks are hard-wired to use technology and social media to the fullest extent. There's nothing wrong with technology if it is used under God's control and for selfless ends.

Lastly, lest you think I forgot about **logistics and location**, I will briefly touch on these issues relative to the super-churches. Most of the senior church leadership and staff at these organizations are very smart and highly-educated individuals. They also understand the importance of campus logistics and efficiency. Their individual church supply chains are run with good quality control. Most seem to be very organized, neat, and smoothly operated. There are many very sincere folks who run these super-church events. Unfortunately, they are sincerely wrong in their approach to a holy and righteous God.

> "Hold fast the form of sound words, which thou hast heard of me, in faith and love which is in Christ Jesus." (2 Timothy 1:13)

What is the impact for the future state of God's Church if we continue down this road?

- If you allow everything, then you stand for nothing.
  - The Word of God must be the only anchor for your life.
  - A holy and righteous approach to godly living is the only approach.
- Pop culture standards become the standards of the church.
  - Buyer beware. You are starting to look just like the world.
- A watered-down version of God's Word and the gospel will not have the impact of penetrating the heart and changing lives.
  - As a result, there will be fewer ministry-minded Christians who are willing to step out by faith and be a part of the ministry.
  - Over time, the lack of ministry participants will hurt the effectiveness of global outreach.

- Longer-lasting spiritual decisions will be few while spur-of-the-moment-church-event affinity will have short-term impact.
  - The Church will become a very transient crowd, always on-the-go and trying to find the perfect church that meets their individual needs.
- Like the major retailers who forced many locally-operated companies out-of-business when they moved into town, small local churches will lack the youth necessary to grow into the future.
  - Small local churches will either shut down or be forced to produce a level of quality that keeps the youth in their current pews. (More on that later)
- A further disintegration of the family unit
  - Grandparents, parents, and children will continue to go their separate ways.
  - The spiritual maturity, wisdom, and education that elders were once able to share with the rest of the family will disappear as the opportunities to minister and influence will be limited.

"That the aged men be sober, grave, temperate, sound in faith, in charity, in patience. The aged women likewise, that they be in behavior as becometh holiness, not false accusers, not given to much wine, teachers of good things; That they may teach the young women to be sober, to love their husbands, to love their children, To be discrete, chaste, keepers at home, good, obedient to their own husbands, that the word of God be not blasphemed." (Titus 2:2-5)

CALL TO ACTION

So what are the next steps for those small- to medium-sized local churches who are trying to have long-term growth in the face of those big-box, retail-type churches? First, they should continue to **preach and teach the whole counsel of God**. Preachers and leaders in the local church must stick to their guns. They must not let their standards diminish even for a second.

Second, they should be willing to **innovate and try new things** to keep the youth interested. I am not suggesting that we should always try to entertain them but find cutting-edge investments that will help them grow and allow them to enjoy learning. Again, I repeat that we should not let down our standards, ever. Stand tall in the face of adversity!

Third, **pray** that God would show you a clear path forward with a vision to create a vibrant local church for the long term. Some of the best youth ministries that I have seen and been involved with developed when their leaders significantly involved themselves in the lives of their students. A balance in age groups will be needed for long-term church growth and maximum evangelistic impact.

> "But strong meat belongeth to them that are of full age, even those who by reason of use have their senses exercised to discern both good and evil." (Hebrews 5:14)

CHRISTIAN LEADERSHIP WORLDVIEW – PRINCIPLE #20

My prayer is that the Christian body of believers will once again become a dynamic community in and through their smaller, local-church bodies. I truly believe that God has given to us this example in the New Testament.

Part 3
Being Led as a Leader

21

PRAYER'S GUIDING INSPIRATION

*"There are many things that are essential to
arriving at true peace of mind,
and one of the most important is faith,
which cannot be acquired without prayer."*
John Wooden

The gift of prayer is such a marvelous and personal way to show praise and complete adoration toward our Lord and Savior, Jesus Christ. Through our willingness to pray, we show Him that we totally and humbly submit ourselves to His perfect authority in our lives.

We first see this spiritual reliance on His authority in the book of *Genesis*. In chapter 4 verse 26, the Bible says,

> "And to Seth, to him also there was born a son; and he called his name Enos: then began men to call upon the name of the Lord."

We are reminded again and again throughout the Word of God that we need a daily time of devotion, a time to die to our old sin nature, to rid ourselves of ourselves, and to be alive in Christ Jesus through intimate and personal prayer with Him. What a wonderful way to begin each precious day, remembering that gift of life that you have been so richly blessed with and to get on your knees and devote yourself to a risen Savior.

- Do you come to Him in **expectant** prayer?
- Do you come **boldly** unto the throne of His grace?

- Do you pray according to His **promises** in the Word of God?
- Do you pray **without ceasing**?
- Do you have a time **alone** with Him each and every day?
- Do you pray to Him during the **good times** as well as during those **wilderness** occasions?
- Do you allow the **Holy Spirit** to direct your prayers?
- Do you **visualize** Jesus Christ listening intently to the concerns of your heart?
- Do you have any **sin** issues that would hinder your time alone with the Lord?
- Do you have a **repentant** attitude before our Savior?
- Is your prayer life **full** with blessing from above or simply an afterthought and a checklist item?
- Are you **specific** with your requests before Him?
- Do you come with **humility**, understanding who He is, the Creator God?
- Is there a spirit of **thanksgiving** for what He has accomplished in you?

"O come, let us worship and bow down: let us kneel before the Lord our maker…" (Psalms 95:6)

"And he was withdrawn from them about a stone's cast, and kneeled down, and prayed." (Luke 22:41)

"And he kneeled down, and cried with a loud voice, Lord, lay not this sin to their charge. And when he had said this, he fell asleep." (Acts 7:60)

CHRISTIAN LEADERSHIP WORLDVIEW – PRINCIPLE #21

If we are being honest with one another, we would admit that praying is a very difficult thing for us to master. It would seem as though there is nothing to it. Right? Each of us should be willing to set time aside every day and go to our Heavenly Father in earnest and expectant prayer. But then, life happens, and our prayer life gets crowded out by the things of this world. We get so "busy" and caught up with the mundane and the trivial that we forget the most important part of our day. Spending time with the Creator God should be the highlight of our day. How are you doing?

22

A Spirit-Filled Imagination

> *"Reason is the natural order of truth;*
> *but imagination is the organ of meaning."*
> *C. S. Lewis*

I praise the Lord that He has given to each of us a special gift through His creation, the intellectual capacity to think about, to meditate on, and to imagine the blessings of our spiritual journey. A Christian's thought life and imagination are extraordinary and powerful gifts in our relationship with our Lord and Savior, Jesus Christ.

During my daily devotionals, I read something that challenged me to consider my thought life and the way I use my imagination. I want to challenge us with the same spiritual encouragement. Do we use our imaginations to put ourselves before a holy and righteous God? Do we use our imaginations when we come boldly unto His throne of grace? Do we use our imaginations when we sing the old-time gospel songs? How about when we pray with our families or participate in local church ministries? Do we use our imaginations for the effectual work of the Lord Jesus Christ?

As a Church body, we need to be continually on guard not to let our worship become thoughtless, unimaginative, and routine. We need to be conscious not to limit ourselves to the ceremonial, the ritual, the formality, and the routine of "playing church." God wants us to use our imaginations for His service, for His worship, and for His praise. If our imaginations and thoughts are not focused on Him, then the things of this earth will grow "strangely brighter", and the natural state of man and his desires will shine through. God does not want us to starve spiritually but simply to imagine Him and the blessings of His glory.

"Lift up your eyes on high, and behold who hath created these things." (Isaiah 40:26)

CHRISTIAN LEADERSHIP WORLDVIEW – PRINCIPLE #22

The ability to use our imaginations can improve one's thought life and greatly add to the excitement of the Christian experience. God has created us in such a unique way that our imaginations can help us give praise and honor to our Heavenly Father in a more meaningful way. Christians need to be willing to explore the boundaries of their God-given imaginations.

23

THE WHOLE COUNSEL OF GOD

"The Bible is one of the greatest blessings bestowed by God on the children of men. It has God for its author; salvation for its end, and truth without any mixture for its matter. It is all pure."
John Locke

What about...   Christ?
What about...   Having a heart for souls?
What about...   Righteous living?
What about...   Instruction from His Word?
What about...   Separation?
What about...   Thirsting for the knowledge of God?

What about...   Justification by Faith?
What about...   Everlasting love?
What about...   Sanctification through His blood?
What about...   Utter dependence on Him?
What about...   Salvation in Christ Jesus?

What about...   Obedience to the calling of God?
What about...   Unity in the body of Christ?
What about...   Rightly dividing the word of truth?

What about... Fasting?
What about... Abiding in that still small place of God?
What about... Total surrender to Him?
What about... His Spirit?
What about... Eternity
What about... Reconciliation with the brethren?

What about... On-going worship and praise of the Savior?
What about... Nourishing the children of God?

What about... Helmet of salvation?
What about... Influencing others through witnessing?
What about... Giving of our time, tithes, and talents?
What about... His righteousness?

What about... **God?**

> **CHRISTIAN LEADERSHIP WORLDVIEW – PRINCIPLE #23**
>
> This acrostic poem was written as a challenge to me personally. It was developed during a time of reflection to survey my own relationship with Christ. It was a time when I considered the lukewarm nature of my existence. In many ways, it was a rebuke for the ways that I thought about spiritual matters. I wanted to hold myself accountable to being someone concerned with the totality of what it means to be a Christian.
>
> While Christianity is certainly not a checklist faith, as we grow in the Lord, we need to ask God to allow the Holy Spirit to broaden our faith and enlarge our capacity to better serve Him.
>
> God continues to use this acrostic in my life to encourage me to pursue new spiritual heights. How will the Lord use me to glorify His name? How will I handle the doctrinal issues described in this acrostic? Will I be disciplined enough to rise to the challenges? I can only pray that the Lord challenges you as He continues to challenge me.

"Turn your eyes upon Jesus, look full in His wonderful face, and the things of earth will grow strangely dim, in the light of His glory and grace."
— Helen H. Lemmel (1922)

24

MOVED WITH COMPASSION

> *"When you pray for anyone, you tend to modify your personal attitude toward him."*
> *Norman Vincent Peale*

When was the last time you were moved with compassion by an individual, event, circumstance, or tragedy? And when you were moved, what did you do about it? What was your course of action to meet the need? How often do those types of moments occur in your life? If our hearts are truly tender toward the things of the Lord, shouldn't we be moved to compassion on a regular basis for the care, concern, and well-being of others?

When you look at our Savior's example, the Bible states in Matthew 14:14 that Jesus **"went forth."** In other words, He was not sitting home in the carpentry shop. Jesus made an effort to be among people. He made a conscious decision to *move toward* those in need.

Likewise, it is our responsibility as Christian leaders to go forth. We must put ourselves in positions to be used for His glory. Too many of us still carry around that old, sin nature and are quite satisfied in the confines and comfort of our "safety" zones. Some call them our "comfort" zones. Many are satisfied to catch an afternoon of "down time" on the couch, or they are simply just not motivated to get something accomplished for the day. I believe that the book of *Proverbs* can be helpful in this area:

> "Go to the ant, thou sluggard; consider her ways, and be wise: Which having no guide, overseer, or ruler, Provideth her meat in the summer, and gathereth her food in the harvest." (Proverbs 6:6-8)

Next, Christ **"saw a great multitude."** Not only did He make the effort to be among the people, when He did, He took notice of their plight. This tells me that there was an active engagement required to notice the needs of others. He went forth with a desire, love, concern, and expectation that people needed what He was offering. Christ wanted to make an impact in the lives of others. He simply anticipated their needs by seeing them with His whole heart.

Thirdly, Christ was **"moved with compassion."** He made the decision to go, to see, and now the experience impacted him spiritually and emotionally. He now felt a burden for the people. He was so deeply moved that he was compelled to do something about it.

Lastly, that compassion toward others propelled Him to act on the behalves of others. **He "healed their sick."** It was within our Savior's power to heal the sick and cause the blind to see. As Christian leaders, it is within your power to step out from behind the podium of "self" to meet the needs of others. How will you demonstrate your love for others? How will you go forth? What are those very first steps that you can take to do the will of the Father?

> "And Jesus *went* forth, and *saw* a great multitude, and was *moved* with compassion toward them, and He *healed* their sick." (Matthew 14:14)

> "But when He *saw* the multitudes, He was *moved* with compassion on them, because they fainted, and were scattered abroad, as sheep having no shepherd." (Matthew 9:36)

REAL WORLD APPLICATION

I decided to combine my reflections on Christ's compassion in Matthew 14 with a drive through an impoverished neighborhood. The two independent experiences allowed me to consider how they could meld into something powerful that could both be a witness for Jesus Christ and help alleviate pain and suffering. I want to share my thought processes of a developed solution as well as the execution methodology for meeting needs.

First, if one is to have a genuine concern for the plight of an impoverished neighborhood, you must be able to **see the need**. Being able to visualize the need means being on the ground level, interacting and building relationships with those that need help. To suggest that one can understand the need by sitting in an office from a distance or even giving generously to a cause without direct involvement would be to miss the point entirely. The most effective leaders make sure they understand their followers' needs. The bottom line is to get involved in the lives of people.

Second, being on the ground level will allow you to build relationships and develop friendships that hopefully will **move you to compassion** for others. Let's call this a desire or burden for a particular individual, group, or even a geographical area. You will be so captivated and moved by the Holy Spirit and for those in need that you have no other choice but to get involved and act. God calls us to specific ministries and groups of people.

Third, having seen the need and being moved and gripped by the opportunity, you **put an action plan in place** to achieve a goal or objective. So the question I pondered is, "What can I do that is within my sphere of influence, credentials, and God given desires and abilities that could make a difference?"

Fourth, you must find that **secret sauce of accountability**. There must be skin in the game from those you are trying to help. I genuinely believe that people want to prosper and succeed. They want to feel like they are making a difference in the world, whatever their station in life and level of society.

That led me directly to my passion, which is leadership training and development. I have been gifted with the ability to teach, motivate, and build the leadership capabilities of others to impact lives. It is my opinion that *Christian Leadership Worldview International* could play a vital role in the local Greenville County area through helping to train and develop tomorrow's leaders. We could do this in less-privileged areas through a variety of organizations and venues. We could do this as part of our existing ministry endeavors. We could help folks reach a whole new level of leadership skill development. Praise God!

CHRISTIAN LEADERSHIP WORLDVIEW – PRINCIPLE #24

Christians have all been blessed with spiritual gifts from above that need to be used for His honor and glory. Our spiritual growth will be hindered if we do not submit and use these gifts to the fullest extent. Be brave. Step out of your comfort zone and get to work. Amazing things will happen!

25

REMEMBER THE MOUNTAINS

> *"Success comes to those who have an entire mountain of gold that they continually mine, not those who find one nugget and try to live on it for fifty years."*
> *John C. Maxwell*

As born-again believers, there are times in our lives when we face spiritual battles and discouragement. It can be difficult as we live and work in this present world's system, exposing ourselves to the constant pounding of Satan and his ways. Each one of us wrestles with the pressures of life and those thorns in the flesh to various degrees, which can hinder our spiritual growth. We continue to be engaged in the world, but at the same time, we are commanded to be separate and not of the world.

Most of us can agree that the Christian walk is one that encompasses both peaks and valleys. Sometimes, we get down and frustrated, spiritually. We become frustrated in that we fall short of His expectations as new creatures in Christ and because our natural man shows through all too often.

Praise the Lord that we can "remember the mountains" when we hit low spots in our spiritual development. Praise the Lord that God's hand of divine protection is always near. If you are discouraged and want God to pick you up spiritually, go to His Word daily, and always "remember the mountains." God uses the description of mountains throughout His Word as examples of His power, His might, and His majesty. He also uses the description of mountains to comfort us, to inspire, and to show us that He is in control.

Here are just a few of the dozens of references in God's Word concerning His mountains.

"As the mountains are round about Jerusalem, so the Lord is round about his people from henceforth even forever." (Psalm 125:2)

"For lo, he that formeth the mountains, and created the wind, and declareth unto man what is his thought, that maketh the morning darkness, and treadeth upon the high places of the earth, The Lord, The God of hosts, is his name." (Amos 4:13)

"Thy righteousness is like the great mountains thy judgments are a great deep: O Lord, thou preservest man and beast." (Psalm 36:6)

"And the mountains shall be molten under him." (Micah 1:4)

"Which by his strength setteth fast the mountains; being girded with power:" (Psalm 65:6)

"He stood and measured the earth: he beheld, and drove asunder the nations; and the everlasting mountains were scattered, the perpetual hills did bow: his ways are everlasting." (Habakkuk 3:6)

"The mountains skipped like rams, and the little hills like lambs." (Psalm 114:4)

> **CHRISTIAN LEADERSHIP WORLDVIEW – PRINCIPLE #25**
>
> God uses the descriptions of mountains in His Word to inspire us, to communicate His power, and to help us appreciate the magnificence of His creation. Praise God!

26
DESIRING OBEDIENCE

> *"We are told to let our light shine, and if it does,*
> *we won't need to tell anybody it does.*
> *Lighthouses don't fire cannons*
> *to call attention to their shining. They just shine."*
> ***Dwight L. Moody***

The process of progressive Christian sanctification happens over a lifetime. The dictionary defines the word *process* as "a series of actions or steps taken in order to achieve a particular end." In the case of Christians, the particular end we strive to achieve is to be more like Christ. We desire for our lives to exude a risen Savior. As we continue to be obedient to His Word—living separate, holy, and righteous lives—we become more and more like our Lord and Savior, Jesus Christ.

First, we must accept Jesus Christ as our Lord and Savior. At the moment we are "adopted" into the family of God and become heirs with Him, the sanctification process begins. For all of mankind, the process of sanctification cannot and will not begin outside of God's call. In short, salvation is the starting point when we accept that free gift from above.

Second, it is through the trials, tribulations, and joys of life that we show obedience to God's Word and are led by the Holy Spirit. There is an ongoing process of being "set apart" or "separate for God's purposes" in this stage of our sanctified development. While we sojourn and are visitors here on earth, Christians are encouraged to draw closer to Him. We do this by being renewed in the Spirit and dying daily to our old sin nature. We desire to put on the mind of Christ. The Lord also will use the circumstances of life to change us and mold us into the image of Christ.

Our old sin nature and the spiritual battles we face are evident as we read through the book of *Romans*.

> "What shall we say then? Shall we continue in sin that grace may abound?" (Romans 6:1)

> "God forbid. How shall we, that are dead to sin, live any longer therein?" (Romans 6:2)

God is telling us to get rid of our former ways of thinking. As easy as it is to hope and pledge to leave that old man behind, we realize just how formidable of a challenge we have. Because we started with a man-centered and sin-filled life, we need to void ourselves from the cares and desires of this evil world. There needs to be much less of ourselves and more of Him. We need to fill our cups with such a reservoir of spiritual water that there is no room left for the natural inclinations of man. When leaders get to the point where they are void of self and full of Him, they can be used greatly for His services.

However, when one holds on to that prideful and self-centered lifestyle, he is a Christian that is unstable in all of his ways. It is as though he wants the blessings of God but desperately tries to hold on to the ways of the world.

Third, the final phase of the sanctification process happens when we go to be with the Lord in Heaven.

> "Now he hath wrought us for the selfsame thing is God, who also hath given unto us the earnest of the Spirit." (2 Corinthians 5:6)

> "For we walk by faith, not by sight." (2 Corinthians 5:7)

"We are confident, I say, and willing rather to be absent from the body, and to be present with the Lord." (2 Corinthians 5:8)

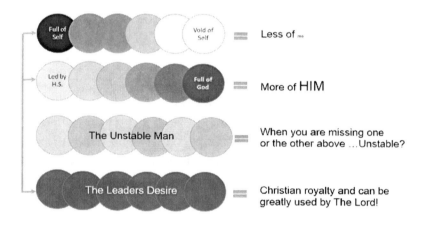

> **CHRISTIAN LEADERSHIP WORLDVIEW – PRINCIPLE #26**
>
> Praise the Lord that we have a hope of a brighter tomorrow in Heaven with Christ! As leaders, we should be aware of our sin nature and desire to crush the old man when it surfaces. An individual with a *Christian leadership worldview* is Spirit-led and disciplined. What a glorious Savior that we serve!

27

TRUST IN ME

> *"I gave in, and admitted that God was God."*
> *C. S. Lewis*

You placed me in this valley vast,
striving to be like Christ at last,
my words, my thoughts, and actions bleak.
Please help me, dear God, for I am weak.

Desires abound with thoughts of You,
yet I stumble and sin and cannot be true.
The Bible, yes, Your words are clear,
but the struggle, dear Lord, is so, so near.

My sin doth beset me and discouraging 'tis.
I wrestle, I am vexed, and I ask, "Why is this?
I placed my faith in Jesus so long ago,
yet the sin, here it is. It continues to show."

Teach me, oh Lord, to rest simply in Thee,
understanding the victory which was Calvary's tree.
So the answer You say, "Finish the race I have set.
Have patience, be loving, for the journey you've met."

"I've sent you the Comforter who resides in your soul,
who gave you much strength when you were made whole
with power on-high to conquer your fears.
For the battle is Mine. The course will I steer."

"Be anxious for nothing, and rest in me still,
for I AM your Savior with a plan. Yes, My will.
In Heaven, we'll meet. Soon enough, it will be.
And you'll shout hallelujah and give glory to Me."

CHRISTIAN LEADERSHIP WORLDVIEW – PRINCIPLE #27

This poem was written to express the enormity and weight of our sin. The Christian is not alone in experiencing the guilt, shame, and exasperation of fighting the old man within. Our old sin nature continues to be a daily struggle and fight. While we rejoice in the free gift of salvation, the course that is set before us is wrought with the complexities and temptations of the natural man. We praise God when the Spirit is leading, but we plead and ask for forgiveness when we stumble and fall.

Oh, to have a God-consciousness every second of every day! Allow the Holy Spirit to consume you. Learn to run the race with patience, knowing that Christ is performing a mighty work. Rest in Him, and trust in Him with your eyes turned to a holy and a sovereign Lord. We have a place called Heaven that is prepared for us. Press forward, and move ahead for the glory of His kingdom. Rejoice in the Savior!

"Fear thou not; for I am with thee: be not dismayed; for I am thy God: I will strengthen thee; yea, I will help thee; yea, I will uphold thee with the right and of my righteousness." (Isaiah 41:10)

28

Failing to Annihilate

"One leak will sink a ship, and one sin will destroy a sinner."
John Bunyan

Throughout the Old Testament, God gave clear directions for what He expected from Israel when they conquered new lands. Whether it was during the time period Israel spent wandering in the wilderness for 40 years under the leadership of Moses or when Joshua led them into the Promised Land, the expectations were the same: total annihilation of the conquered the lands.

At first glance, one might think this decision was just a little rough and over the top. Did God really mean to "utterly destroy" and annihilate? Yes, that is exactly what He meant!

> "Then ye shall drive out all the inhabitants of the land from before you, and destroy all their pictures, and destroy all their molten images, and quite pluck down all their high places." (Numbers 33:52)

> "But the Lord thy God shall deliver them unto thee, and shall destroy them with a mighty destruction, until they be destroyed."
> (Deuteronomy 7:23)

> "Ye shall utterly destroy all the places, wherein the nations which ye shall possess served their gods, upon the high mountains, and upon the hills, and under every green tree: And ye shall overthrow their altars, and break their pillars, and burn their groves

> with fire; and ye shall hew down the graven images of their gods, and destroy the names of them out of that place." (Deuteronomy 12:2-3)

God wanted them free from the temptations of sin and the potential association with worldliness and wicked devices. He wanted them focused on Him with all of their heart, mind, and soul. Our Lord understood that this would not be possible if the noise and clutter of the present world were allowed in. God knows our human nature, predispositions, and weaknesses. In the Old Testament days, God understood what the "mixed multitude" would represent in the long-term. The seeds of corruption, wickedness, lies, apostasy, and idolatry would taint a "peculiar people" who were set apart for a specific purpose. He even went so far as to explain what would happen if they failed to obey. To explain that disobedience would bring uncommon misery, heartache, and ruin.

> "Else if you do in any wise go back, and cleave unto the remnant of these nations, even these that remain among you, and shall make marriages with them, and go in unto them, and they to you: Know for a certainty that the Lord your God will no more drive out any of these nations from before you; but they shall be snares and traps unto you, and scourges in your sides, and thorns in your eyes, until ye perish from off this good land which the Lord your God hath given you." (Joshua 22:12-13)

Let us now make some practical application to our lives as we live out our faith in the 21st century. From the previous verses, we know that God hates sin, wants our obedience, gives us guidance, sends early warning, and will correct us with His loving hands of righteousness when needed. Is there application today for *failing to annihilate*? Yes, there certainly is! Please read on.

We absolutely are NOT talking about murder or the annihilation of any particular race, culture, religious group, or region of the world. No, we are talking about the annihilation of the sin within each of our hearts. There are several questions that we can ask ourselves in this regard (relating to sin) to draw the appropriate conclusions.

- Are you willing to annihilate the passions, lusts, and possessions of this world that put you in positions of temptation?
- Are you willing to annihilate all evil thoughts and everything that stands in the way of you doing the will of God?
- Are you willing to annihilate those things that inhibit the full, complete, and expansive working of the Holy Spirit?
- What about your spiritual gifts? Are you willing to annihilate the fears, narcissism, and self-consciousness of how you might look in the eyes of the world by exercising those gifts? In other words, are you willing to set aside what the world might think of you?
- What about all of the human inhibitions that hold you back from witnessing, teaching, and taking an activist position for the Lord in what is pure, just, holy, and right?

The list of questions could go on and on. Each one of us that peers into His Word on a daily basis clearly understands the message. The real bottom line question is this: *How committed are you to the annihilation of worldly lusts?* Are you so entangled with the pleasures of this world and its system that there is no "turning back" to the purity of fundamental Christianity? Do you have the discipline, focus, determination, love, and compassion for the things of God to annihilate those sin issues that hold you back?

Together, as a family in Christ Jesus, I believe we can hold each other accountable to fight evil and root out the sin that so easily besets us. While we will never see perfection this side of heaven, we must fight the good fight and run the race that is set before us. Right now, what are you *failing to annihilate* for the glory of God?

CHRISTIAN LEADERSHIP WORLDVIEW – PRINCIPLE #28

The sin in our lives is not something we should take lightly. If not addressed, it will crowd out the joy that we have in Christ Jesus. We should be at full attention and on guard against the sins of this world. Christians must be diligent in rooting out and annihilating their respective sins that so easily beset them.

29

A SPIRIT-FILLED CHURCH

> *"The revealed Word awakened me, but it was the preached Word that saved me, and I must ever attach peculiar value to the hearing of the truth, for by it I received the joy and peace in which my soul delights."*
> **Charles Spurgeon**

Jesus Christ desires for His children to yield completely and willingly to the leading of the Holy Spirit of God. Like a father leading his children, He wants us to listen, obey, and then put into action what He has commanded. In yielding, we place ourselves in a position where individually we can be used to stir and revive hearts. While revival is a work that God alone must perform in mankind, by yielding to the Holy Spirit, we can be used as instruments for the furtherance of the gospel message and for His good pleasure.

The word, *revival*, in the Greek in many instances literally means "to come back from the dead." In order for God to revive the hearts of wicked men, several evidences must be present. F. Carlton Booth writes, "Revival always involves the preaching of divine judgment, confession of sin, repentance, acceptance of salvation as a free gift, the authority of the Scriptures, and the joy and discipline of the Christian life."

When we look at our individual church bodies in relation to the evidences of revival, do we see these manifestations in our midst? As a church body, do we see souls being saved, people confessing their sins, desiring to live disciplined Christian lives, while focusing on pleasing their Lord and Savior, Jesus Christ? I believe we do! And if revival means "to come back from the dead", isn't our Lord pleased with the salvation and the conversion of just one soul? Luke 15:7 states,

> "I say unto you, that likewise joy shall be in heaven over one sinner that repenteth, more than over ninety and nine just persons, which need no repentance."

While discussing the importance of living a disciplined Christian life, we may look among our church body and thank the Lord for the wonderful and dedicated members who truly desire to serve Him. We have people in our church who are being called to the ministry, young folks that are preaching God's Word, members desiring to care one for another, and many of the other manifestations that Carlton Booth expressed.

I ask you again, do we have revival in our midst? If you are waiting for revival to be some emotional out-of-body human experience, then we would agree to disagree. However, if you believe that revival is seeing souls saved and seeing Christians yielded to His Word with a fresh desire, then I don't think you have to look any further than to your brother and sister in Christ sitting right next to you in church. Praise God in the Highest! Please, stir our hearts, dear Lord!

CHRISTIAN LEADERSHIP WORLDVIEW – PRINCIPLE #29

Yes, I believe that God is going to send another revival to our country. It will happen when Christians start praying for the spiritual rebirth of the nation. I truly believe that God is not finished with the United States of America. His patient and long-suffering nature is currently on display. When the time is right (perfect), He will intercede.

30

DISCERNING SIN'S ALLURE

"The god of this world is riches, pleasure, and pride."
Martin Luther

Consider your sin. Can we stop and reflect for a moment on the impact and effects of our sin?

THE EARTHLY PERSPECTIVE

In human terms, sin can't be that bad. Can it? I really didn't mean it. I said I was sorry. It is just not that much of a big deal. It was a lie, an oversight, and a small exaggeration here and there. I don't think I hurt anyone. So I exaggerated the numbers a little with my boss; everyone does it to tell their own story and to get their projects approved. In the scope of things, my small sins are not the end of the world. My cheating, lying, drinking, and stealing are just part of the world we live in. I am not as bad as the murderers on death row and behind bars. Just chill out and relax. I'm not going to get caught. No big deal.

THE HEAVENLY PERSPECTIVE

We have been created by a holy and righteous God. We live in a spiritual world where the powers of Satan are evident. He is the prince of this world. Satan wants to overthrow the Holy One of the universe.

> "Be sober, be vigilant; because your adversary the devil, as a roaring lion, walketh about, seeking whom he may devour." (1 Peter 5:8)

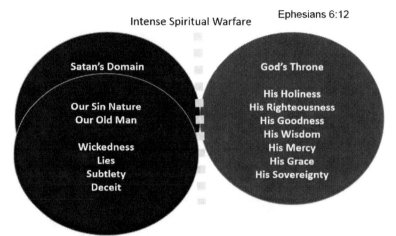

Satan is trying to encroach upon the throne of God and his absolute authority

Satan is basically trying to de-throne and discredit our Lord and Savior Jesus Christ

With our disobedience, our sin nature, and our lust after the natural man, aren't we doing the exact same thing?

Leaders must be aware of what their sin represents

CHRISTIAN LEADERSHIP WORLDVIEW – PRINCIPLE #30

Christians must understand the lasting impact of their sin and what it represents. Your sinful actions are attempts to encroach the throne of God… just as Satan does.

31

DESPERATE NEED

"We are always on the anvil; by trials God is shaping us for higher things."
Henry Ward Beecher

I started to think about the phrase, "desperate need", from a spiritual perspective and wondered why I fall short. Why is it that I am not driven to the cross of Calvary like my forefathers of the 17th century? Why don't I have a compassion and a zeal for the spiritual state of others like I should?

As a society, have we become so complacent with the things of the Lord and so self-absorbed that we feel nothing? We have our health. We have our safety. We have our food. We have our prosperity. We worship freely without fear of persecution (for the most part). For all of these things, we should be grateful. Are we grateful? What is it going to take in the 21st century to drive Christians to their knees in the *desperate need* of the Lord? What are the circumstances of life that either will wake us up individually or as a nation?

Like the second- and third-generation Puritans, it appears that we have become hypnotized with the prosperity of this world. We have it all. Why do we need the Lord? Are we so self-sufficient that we crowd out the things of the Lord?

> "For because thou hast trusted in thy works and in thy treasures, thou shalt also be taken: and Chemosh shall go forth into captivity with his priests and his princes together." (Jeremiah 48:7)

> **CHRISTIAN LEADERSHIP WORLDVIEW – PRINCIPLE #31**
>
> Let it be the prayer of Christians that we never become so self-absorbed, self-satisfied, and self-reliant that we do not *desperately* seek the Lord. Please, Lord, bring us to our knees!

32

IN HIS PRESENCE

> *"May we have communion with God in the secret of our hearts, and find Him to be to us as a little sanctuary."*
> **Charles Spurgeon**

I yearn for His presence to be lovingly near.
Our Master, our Savior, it is Him we do fear.
That still small place is so precious to me
to commune with Christ Jesus, Great Counselor is He.

One day, up in Heaven, in awe will we stand.
In a moment, a shout, He'll reach for our hand.
That day we know not, that time unrevealed.
As children of God, our souls have been sealed.

Try Him, and search Him, and you'll find Him close by.
In His presence we rejoice, Our Savior on high.
God's Word is so powerful, so beautiful, and so clear.
It is there you will find Him. Just ask. He will hear.

His words are convicting yet so marvelous and true.
At times, we see the natural man. At times, we feel brand new.
These words of His give joy and life and health to our bones.
God's Word will bring Him closer still 'til the time we go home.

So I say to God's children from the depths of my soul…
continue in His presence 'til the time you grow old.
For to know Him and walk with Him is a gift from above.
In His presence, we will experience the power of His love.

CHRISTIAN LEADERSHIP WORLDVIEW – PRINCIPLE #32

This poem was written as a challenge to Christians (primarily to me) to stay disciplined and continue to seek the things of the Lord. When you seek the love and guidance of our Lord, you always will find Him available. If you have a true and sincere yearning for the things from above, God will answer your spiritual desires.

However, as Christians, we must remember that God hates our sin. If we are truly going to find that "still, small place" of the Lord and continue to be filled with His Spirit, it will take a special, disciplined effort to rid ourselves of those natural, fleshly desires.

This course of life is truly a long-distance race and not a sprint. We must challenge ourselves to stay the course for His glory in this spiritual journey of life. Heaven is waiting, a victor's crown to receive. There are two verses of scripture that come to mind:

"Set your affection on things above, not on things on the earth." (Colossians 3:2)

"For in this we groan, earnestly desiring to be clothed upon with our house which is from heaven." (2 Corinthians 5:2)

Part 4

A Leader Sees God in Everyday Living

33

The Two-Sided Fence

by Lauren LaPierre

"Tell me and I forget. Teach me and I remember. Involve me and I learn."
Benjamin Franklin

As a young girl growing up on a small farm, I often observed our numerous animals. We owned six ornery geese, each of which possessed a surprisingly endearing name. Gem, Diamond, Ruby, Emerald, Sparkle, and White Feather were all grouped in a huddle one particular day on the other side of a metal fence that contained them. They were tall and almost pretty creatures as they jumped in and out of an old bathtub that contained water provided by a hose. They would splash and honk and create such a noise that it was quite impossible to ignore the ruckus.

I decided to stop and admire these God-created animals on a sunny, fall afternoon. It was leaf-raking season, and I needed a break from the constant back-and-forth motion. These boisterous pets glared at me with their pairs of beady eyes and long, cocked necks. I dropped my rake down on the browning grass and started stepping closer and closer to the fence. I crouched down as I got nearer to the barrier. Before I knew it, my nose was just barely peeking through the fence.

Sometimes, things happen so fast that there's barely time to process them in order to react. This was one of those moments. I froze in my tracks, surrounded by a pile of leaves. In a fast flutter of feathers, a goose was charging straight at me, beak first. I never realized geese possessed teeth until the moment one gripped the tip of my nose! The pain of the attack sunk in quickly as I jumped back as fast as I could. I think I might have resembled Rudolph the Red-Nosed Reindeer for several hours after.

Much like I kept creeping toward that fence, it is easy for Christians to become distracted by things that look exciting and appealing. The problem is that the distraction can take our attention away from what is pure and toward that which can cause harm spiritually. If I hadn't taken my eyes off of my work and what I was supposed to be accomplishing, I would not have been entrapped in a painful situation. The Bible says,

> "Love not the world, neither the things that are in the world. If any man love the world, the love of the Father is not in him. For all that is in the world, the lust of the flesh, and the lust of the eyes, and the pride of life, is not of the Father, but is of the world." (1 John 2:15-16)

Little did I know that, throughout this entire episode, Dad was standing behind me, watching the entire show unfold. He could have intervened and forced me to move away from the fence. In this case, however, his wisdom guided him to have me learn a lesson through experience. The only way I was going to avoid a precarious situation was to stay away from it. As soon as the bite ensued, Dad started laughing quite heartily at my predicament. At the time, I saw no humor in the situation, but as I write this now, I cannot stop smiling.

He could have said, "I told you so", because he told me to stand back from the fence and the geese many times before. But what he said to me has applied to so many areas in my life. He said, "Now you know for next time not to get close to the fence."

This lesson has applied to my spiritual life often. I need to avoid what drags me away from my relationship with God because it can only be detrimental. No matter how tantalizing something sounds, how beautiful it looks, or how fun it seems, if it draws me away from God toward what is wrong in His sight, I must redirect my focus to make the right decisions. Only then will my spiritual life be beautiful.

CHRISTIAN LEADERSHIP WORLDVIEW – PRINCIPLE #33

There are even teaching moments through what I will call "barnyard theology"! The circumstances and events of life that are seen through the eyes of a child can be quite impressionable. Parents should never underestimate the impact that ordinary events can have in the life of a child. Christians should learn to use and cherish each of these moments. They bring both learning and laughter!

34

THIS OLD HOUSE

"You can see God from anywhere if your mind is set to love and obey Him."
Aiden Wilson Tozer

My wife and I hopped in a car,
a countryside wanting to see,
long, winding roads that took us afar
with no thought of our destiny.

Sitting back, taking in heaven's display,
this glorious creation of His:
green pastures, high mountains, and farms in array,
swaying trees bending back in the wind.

And while we drove, what came in view?
This splendid little place:
a porch, a barn, and gardens, too…
Sweet vegetables to taste.

But drawing near, we were aghast.
The sight we did behold
with chimney gone, foundation cracked…
this house for sale we're told.

We peeked inside and saw those rooms,
all sheet rock falling down.
I called to my wife, "Let's grab the brooms.
This duty we are bound."

For when God calls, we cannot wait.
Much work to be done.
Give Me thine heart and observe My ways.
All glory to My Son.

Linoleum torn and rugs thread-bare,
with shingles on the ground
in such a state of disrepair,
Christ's project have we now.

With stain-cracked doors and window frames
and water all around…
"Lord, why this house?" we both exclaimed.
A worst could not be found.

"For this old house will be like new.
You'll see someday, I'm sure.
Some faith, your prayers and patience, too…
My tabernacle to restore."

"A strong foundation is what I've said.
My cornerstone is the need.
I sent My Son in your stead
to take your place indeed."

This spiritual lesson have we been taught.
With discerning eyes, we see.
Showy exteriors are good for naught,
a sturdy foundation to leave.

A Sunday drive again we'll take.
Another house to build,
willing channels for His sake,
knowing, "I am God… be still."

CHRISTIAN LEADERSHIP WORLDVIEW – PRINCIPLE #34

This poem was written as an allegory to encourage believers not to be focused on the outward appearance of man. There will be times in our lives when Christ, in His perfect timing, will allow us the privilege to encounter and minister to those who are not just like us. Therefore, don't let the shell and the exterior of people in your "chance" encounters in life negatively impact your duties and responsibilities as a Christian.

Because Christ wants us to participate in many of these spiritual restoration projects, as godly instruments for His service, we should be open, receptive, and grateful for each opportunity. As a matter of fact, God wants us and expects us to be on the lookout for those in need.

"Redeeming the time because the days are evil..." (Ephesians 5:16)

"So shall my word be that goeth forth out of my mouth; it shall not return unto me void, but it shall accomplish that which I please, and it shall prosper in the thing whereto I sent it." (Isaiah 55:11)

"And the things that thou hast heard of me among many witnesses, the same commit thou to faithful men, who shall be able to teach others also." (2 Timothy 2:2)

35

Handfuls of Purpose

"God never made a promise that was too good to be true."
Dwight L. Moody

The veil of His temple miraculously rent,
our glorious Savior to us He was sent.
That gift of salvation so rich and so free,
a poor, rescued sinner who looked just like me.

Providing this manna on-high from above,
provisions expressing His wonderful love.
Pure, living waters designed to sustain,
Abundantly deep, a spiritual plane.

The Spirit of God desiring to lead,
His promises written which I now believe.
Absolute truth in Him do we find,
lovingly bestowed to all of mankind.

Great mercy and grace which He freely gives,
with the "fruit of the Spirit" His will to live.
His longsuffering nature in us to surround,
"in the shadow of my wings", it's there you'll be found.

Shelter, much food, with raiment have we,
Heaven's home prepared, a place that we'll be.
Worries are gone, no doubts and no fear,
coming from heaven, a voice that we hear.

With absolute safety and sweet peaceful rest,
trust in the Savior, it is there we are blessed.
Handfuls of purpose in Ruth do we read,
the eloquence of expression, His wisdom is seen.

CHRISTIAN LEADERSHIP WORLDVIEW – PRINCIPLE #35

This poem was written to reflect on the endless number of gifts and blessings that God bestows upon us daily. These blessed gifts range from the spiritual, physical, and the material. He has given to us the free gift of salvation. He provides for our physical needs. He provides for our spiritual needs. He provides for our needs relating to food, shelter, and clothing. Oh, what a heavenly Father we have who is intimately concerned about the needs of His children. Fortunately, those concerns do not end with the passing of time here on earth. He has prepared a home for us in heaven above. He has revealed Himself in His Word through the Spirit of God and through His wonderful creation. As we hide in the shadow of His wings, we will come to exude the characteristics of a holy and righteous God.

36
GOD'S LIGHTNING STRIKES

"Salvation is from our side a choice, from the divine side it is a seizing upon, an apprehending, a conquest by the Most High God. Our 'accepting' and 'willing' are reactions rather than actions. The right of determination must always remain with God."
Aiden Wilson Tozer

I want to challenge every Christian leader to dig in and fully explore the "Great Awakening" period in the history of the United States of America. It was a period when God's Word penetrated the hearts and souls of Christians and non-Christians alike. Yes, there have been several other occasions when our country has experienced a spiritual awakening. However, the period starting around 1733-1734 saw the Holy Spirit work in ways that only a sovereign, holy, and righteous God could manifest. When we reflect back and see how God literally brought thousands upon thousands of lost souls to a saving knowledge of Jesus Christ, we can only stand amazed. His work changed the fabric of our country during this time period. People started getting right with the Lord, which made an impact on families, communities, and even whole regions of the country.

The Bible talks a lot about the sovereign power of God and how He rules on high. God is in control.

> "He hath made the earth by his power, he hath established the world by his wisdom, and hath stretched out the heaven by his understanding." (Jeremiah 51:15)

"Who hath wrought and done it, calling the generations from the beginning? I the Lord, the first, and the last, I am he." (Isaiah 41:4)

"Lift up your eyes on high, and behold who hath created these things, that bringeth out their host by number: he calleth them all by names by the greatness of his might, for that he is strong in power; not one faileth." (Isaiah 40:26)

"For he knoweth our frame." (Psalm 103:14)

"His eyes behold the nations." (Psalm 66:7)

"Doth not he see my ways, and count all my steps?" (Job 31:4)

God used men in the illustration below along with a confluence of other factors to impact our country for Jesus Christ.

- Our nation had just left a period of brutal Indian uprisings and massacres.
- A new generation of preachers were preaching a salvation message that ripped to the heart of man and brought repentence.
- The British throne was putting tremendous pressure on the colonists.
- Disease, sickness, and the death rate were still at uncontrollable levels.
- Gifted leaders were willing to be used as instruments for God's good pleasure during the "Great Awakening" period.

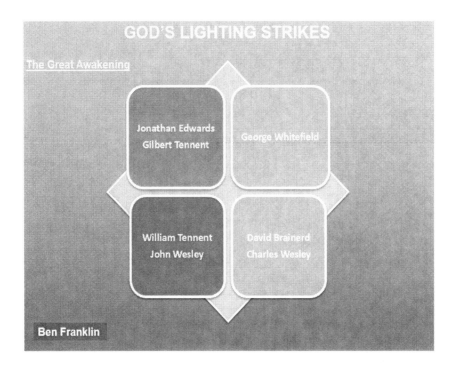

CHRISTIAN LEADERSHIP WORLDVIEW – PRINCIPLE #36

From time to time, Christian leaders need to take a look back at our country's history. Those who seek to be leaders need to understand the role that our Christian forefathers played in the development of our country. We must not get sucked into the revisionist view of American's founding.

37

THOSE PESKY LITTLE FELLAS

"If you are not allowed to laugh in heaven, I don't want to go there."
Martin Luther

We traveled to Maine, such a beautiful coast,
enjoying God's creation, the beaches the most.
York Beach was the spot in which we did stay,
a tourist's delight with no work and all play.

So relaxing and peaceful, a place such as this.
Only days do we have, this town will be missed.
Towels wrapped around, running down to the shore,
can't waste a minute, busting through the camp's door.

Positioning our blankets, we bathed in the sun,
not a care in the world, such a blast, so much fun.
But all of a sudden, a noise did we hear,
a swarm of blackflies, so we ran just like deer.

We came back around a few minutes I'd say.
Still plenty of time, we have most of the day.
Back in our comfort as we lay on the beach,
writing some poems, a sermon to preach.

But then, once again, that strange buzzing sound.
An itch, yes, a scratch… those black flies are around.
Some call them, *no-see-ems*, so irritating are they.
A swat and a slap to chase them away.

Blood-sucking little creatures, no use I can tell.
For sure, they'll be in that place we call hell.
Swarming and darting, they bite their way through,
leaving bumps on my skin, big pockmarks there, too.

So we put on the lotion, burning incense we must,
in the morning, at noon, all the way until dusk.
On guard do we stand, a fervent spirit have we.
Those pesky little fellas will soon die. You'll see.

The Lord our Creator has designed them for you.
Oh, no. It can't be. It must not be true.
Please do them no harm. They're part of God's plan.
They clean up the beaches, the rocks, and the sand.

All refuse and things that have died long ago
are removed by those flies. I'm afraid it is so.
So you're saying to me my attitude should change
toward blood-sucking hoodlums? Seems a bit strange.

So, I'll give it a try. A cease-fire we'll call,
marking our territories, an understanding is all.
I have great misgivings this peace will not last.
Then again, if it doesn't, I sure can run fast.

CHRISTIAN LEADERSHIP WORLDVIEW – PRINCIPLE #37

This poem was written with a three-fold purpose in mind. First, I wanted to thank the Lord for the beauty of His creation. It was a simple expression of admiration for the small, intricate details that we find here on earth. To show how God in His infinite wisdom and sovereign power is able to design and choreograph the magnificence of the most micro-elements in nature, an ecosystem that only a Creator God is capable of perfecting!

Second, it was written with just a touch of good 'ole "Maine" humor. Any true "Mainer" undoubtedly has experienced the impact of this subject matter. Well, you will get the gist.

Third, it is to demonstrate that having a *Christian leadership worldview* means to see the Lord in every aspect of life. We want to thank Him when we laugh, while basking in His creation, or even when vacationing with family and friends. As Christian leaders, we desperately need a God-consciousness throughout every minute of every day! Praise God!

38

THOSE STORM CLOUDS YONDER

> *"We are not diplomats but prophets,*
> *and our message is not a compromise but an ultimatum."*
> *Aiden Wilson Tozer*

Those storm clouds are gathering
off in the distant sky,
God's power and His majesty
displayed right there on high.

Those ominous, foreboding clouds
with radiant hues of gray,
the lightning flash, and thunder, too,
will come your way today.

Those storm clouds are gathering.
You sense your day is near.
"So much to do. Not now," you say.
In Him I cannot fear.

Through blind eyes, I see the world
with no thought of you,
these moments of life, simply passing by.
It's sad, I know, but true.

Those storm clouds are gathering.
This life so fast a pace,
running here and there and everywhere.
Let's go. We must make haste.

So oblivious to life's meaning now,
you hear those crushing sounds.
You ask if this is meant for you,
no answer to be found.

Those storm clouds are gathering.
New life we hope to see.
Christian channels, yes, do witness still.
They shout salvation's plea.

But as those clouds do now approach,
His will we now understand.
The planks, the nails, the gallows built,
we wait for His command.

Those gallows' planks completed now,
the appointment came so soon.
Still time to call the Savior,
His Son for you to choose.

And as he walks those planks of death,
Christian channels again appear.
Just ask they cry, "Believe in Him,"
He will remove all fears.

The hangman asks just one more time,
"What do you have to say?"
He begs and pleads for this lost soul
to be with Him today.

No, I say, this life I've led
is mine to proclaim.
I will not, cannot, bow to Him.
My answer is the same.

My pride, the arrogance is who I am.
For me to take a knee
is to admit my sinful ways.
In this, I shall not heed.

The Christian channels cried and wept.
They knew what lay ahead.
A meeting with our glorious Maker…
the Book, his name not read.

The hood, the rope… it tightens now…

CHRISTIAN LEADERSHIP WORLDVIEW – PRINCIPLE #38

This poem was written as a challenge to those who are not followers of Jesus Christ. It is an allegory using the storm clouds of God's creation against a backdrop of the gallows of eternal damnation. The hope is to depict those who are consumed with the busyness and cares of this life and who never stop to reflect and enjoy its true Christ-centered meaning.

Life and all of its pleasures surround and control us. This world wants to monopolize our thoughts, desires, and actions to the point where there is no room for anything else. Through the passage of time, the spiritual storm clouds start to move closer still. Christians beckon and plead the cause of Christ to those in need but to no avail. The gallows now stand ready to receive their own.

"But thou didst trust in thine own beauty, and playedst the harlot because of thy renown, and pouredst out thy fornications on everyone that passed by; his it was." (Ezekiel 16:15)

"Therefore shall they eat of the fruit of their own way, and be filled with their own devices." (Proverbs 1:31)

39

THE JOY OF LIFE

"There is a power in God's gospel beyond all description."
Charles Spurgeon

Dear Heavenly Father and Lord, Master above,
I feel your presence and sense your great love.
I wake up each morning and give you the praise
and shout, "Hallelujah!", for I know I am saved.

This moment of life is so precious to me,
and I thank you, dear Lord, for setting me free.
Deserving I'm not and wicked am I,
yet one day I'll meet you in Heaven on-high.

To seek after You is more precious than gold.
In the Word… in the Psalms… it is there I am told
You'll love us and will keep us from the enemy and strife
if we only follow You with all diligence and all might.

I beg you, dear God, keep my paths straight ahead,
and let me not wander, for I know what you've said.
It is but sin for a season and joy that will flee.
"Keep your eyes upon the Savior and, in turn, upon Me."

It is the power of the cross where your love is now shown.
This spirit that rests within me is Yours and Yours alone.
The miracle on Mount Calvary I dare not understand,
for, Lord, I am only human and accept this gift as your plan.

Until that great day when we meet in the sky,
let me praise you, my Father, 'til the day that I die.
This *joy of life* that I experience each day
is but a gift from Thee, Your hands and the clay.

CHRISTIAN LEADERSHIP WORLDVIEW – PRINCIPLE #39

This poem was written to give complete praise and adoration to our Lord and Savior, Jesus Christ. It is an expression of gratitude for who He is and His willingness to go to the cross of Calvary. It is a reflection of a world that was wonderfully created by a loving and merciful God.

This poem also reminds us of our responsibility to seek His face in the Word of God and to be committed to following a straight path ahead spiritually.

"Praise ye the Lord. Praise God in his sanctuary: praise him in the firmament of his power. Praise him for his mighty acts: praise him according to his excellent greatness. Praise him with the sound of the trumpet: praise him with the psaltery and harp. Praise him with the timbrel and dance: praise him with stringed instruments and organs. Praise him upon the loud cymbals: praise him upon the high-sounding cymbals. Let everything that hath breath praise the Lord. Praise ye the Lord." (Psalm 150:1-6)

Part 5
Leading as a Parent

40

A Parent's Roadmap

"In giving us children, God places us in a position of both leadership and service. He calls us to give up our lives for someone else's sake — to abandon our own desires and put our child's interests first. Yet, according to His perfect design, it is through this selflessness that we can become truly fulfilled."
Charles Stanley

Very early in our marriage, a very kind and generous soul once asked me how our children were turning out so well. What was the key ingredient that helped my wife and me along the way? As I contemplated those questions over the next 30 minutes, I realized that what they were actually asking was something quite different than what they had verbalized. What they really wanted to know was the "secret sauce" of childrearing I could share that would make all of their problems disappear.

Well, we all know that it doesn't quite work that way. There is much trial and error as new parents, and it is only by the leading of the Holy Spirit that childrearing can be accomplished.

The man who asked the question and his wife were going through some challenging times with their children and truly were looking for some good, biblical answers to their questions. I could tell by their expressions that it was not going to be a casual conversation. They were locked onto every word I spoke that day.

Quite frankly, the conversation took me aback. Who was I to offer any type of advice to those who seemed to be much more experienced and spiritual? I was a very immature Christian. As I look back at my fumbled answers to their many questions, I now realize that I could have offered much deeper and wider spiritual counsel on the subject. If I remember correctly, I gave them a few tips (from my inexperience and youth) that I hoped would help them along the way. These were crucial to me at the time. It was real basic stuff.

- Keep them in the Bible.
- Love them.
- Be a disciplinarian.

Well, that was basically all I had to offer. I truly felt self-conscious about sharing this advice because I felt terribly inadequate as a parent. I was much too impatient, had somewhat of a quick temper, and always wanted things done my way… right away. My children probably felt like they were in Christian boot camp! Truly, my wife was our better half in the childrearing department.

But one thing is for sure; they knew without question that we loved them and would care for them at any cost. We told them that we loved them every single day while they were growing up. In my mind, there is no doubt that our children knew we loved them.

I praise God that our children have turned out as they have. They are three Christian adults willing to serve the Lord and are contributing to society at large. Sinners saved by the grace of God.

While on the surface, everything I said that day in the way of encouragement and counsel was on target, reflecting back as a grandparent, I would elaborate even more. I would encourage our children (with our grandchildren) to contemplate the gift they have been given in a deeper and more meaningful, spiritual way. Of course, the Word of God would still be the starting point and the anchor for any and all childrearing instructions.

> "And, ye fathers, provoke not your children to wrath: but bring them up in the nurture and admonition of the Lord." (Ephesians 6:4)

> "Foolishness is bound in the heart of a child; but the rod of correction shall drive it far from him." (Proverbs 22:15)
>
> "For whosoever shall call upon the name of the Lord shall be saved." (Romans 10:13)
>
> "Thou shalt love the Lord thy God with all thy heart, and with all thy soul, and with all thy mind." (Matthew 22:37)
>
> "But the fruit of the spirit is love, joy, peace, longsuffering, gentleness, goodness, faith, meekness, temperance: against such there is no law." (Galatians 5:22-23)
>
> "Therefore all things whatsoever ye would that men should do to you, do ye even so to them: for this is the law and the prophets." (Matthew 7:12)

And with these verses as the solid rock and parenting foundation, I would offer the following thoughts, insights, and advice in the Lord.

1. Love them.
2. Correct them.
3. Provide for them.
4. Encourage them.
5. Acknowledge the Lord's sovereign power in their lives.
6. Diligently run the race.
7. Lead a disciplined Christian life as an example.
8. Ask for forgiveness when you make a mistake.
9. Have fun and enjoy them.
10. Love them.

Yes, the bookends are by design: love them. I hope that, in some small way, this tidbit of advice can help you become the parent that God wants you to be. Please do not look at our example as the model for parenting. Please look to the Bible. Thank you, Lord, for our children and grandchildren!

CHRISTIAN LEADERSHIP WORLDVIEW – PRINCIPLE #40

The responsibilities of being a parent are monumental. Only through biblical instruction and guidance can the ultimate source and foundation of absolute truth be instilled in our children's lives. Human reasoning, conjecture, logic, and earthly wisdom will produce children with no spiritual depth or insight.

41

LOVING YOUR CHILDREN THROUGH LETTERS

> *"For victory in life, we've got to keep focused on the goal, and the goal is Heaven."*
> **Lou Holtz**

Dear Lauren Rose,

Upon the deepest reflection and contemplation in writing this celebratory note to our sweetest, dearest, Lauren Rose, we find ourselves in a state betwixt two: the one, praising God and thanking Him for the work He has begun in you in shaping your spiritual character and moral strength; the other, hopelessly saddened by the thought of your absence for a time. The joy that you brought into our lives on a daily basis can't be replaced.

Yet, we know that the will of God and higher education beckons, and we look forward with eager anticipation of what HE has planned for your life. We sincerely will miss seeing you every day. These ever-present sentiments are emotions that we now have encountered for a third and final time. Yet, the departure of a daughter is severely more perplexing than the previous. The need, I suppose, is the desire to protect the weaker vessel. Certainly not weak in intellect or strength of spirit but as it relates to the physical makeup and stature of the female gender.

Oh, what a joy it has been to watch you grow in the Lord through the years. A little baby, a toddler (yes, that would be those terrific twos), a young girl, a teenager, and now a young woman equipped to face the challenges that lie ahead. When we think back over your development, the one thing that is immensely vivid in our minds is the softness of your heart. It has been both an inspiration and a rebuke to your parents. For when we think of the person that you have become, we need only look to the Holy Scriptures and the evidence of the fruit of the Spirit as shown in Galatians: love, joy, peace, longsuffering, gentleness, goodness, faith, meekness, and temperance are all characteristics of our Lord and Savior, Jesus Christ, that have clearly become part of your being. As such, we encourage you to get on your knees and ask the Lord to continue to fill you with His Spirit each day.

And now, as you go off to college and leave us for a time, if we may be so bold as to offer you some loving guidance and instruction.

As it relates to advice on the future bond of marriage, diligently seek the Lord. And yes, soon, all too soon, you will have the privilege of meeting the man that our God has chosen for you as a help-meet. In this determination, you must be the wiser. If a young man has pledged his love for you and is most inclined to take you as his bride, and you in turn share those same feelings, then his love must include an understanding of your need to complete those things that you have set out to accomplish. In this determination, you must also be patient, for the suitors will be many, accepting godly counsel from your family and the people who love you most.

As it relates to advice on your spiritual gifts, diligently seek the Lord. The gift of music, the love of children, the gift of helps, and the gift of compassion should be exercised in their totality.

As it relates to advice on your friends, diligently seek the Lord. Through much prayer, have the courage to surround yourself with people who will build you up in the faith. Remember that iron sharpeneth iron.

And finally, while you are off at college experiencing this newfound freedom of yours, make sure you take the time to enjoy yourself. Study as you must, but we say again, take lots of time to enjoy the college experience.

Lauren Rose, we love you. May God strengthen you in the Spirit, guide your steps, and keep you safe until you return to us again.

With love from your adoring parents,
Mom & Dad

CHRISTIAN LEADERSHIP WORLDVIEW – PRINCIPLE #41

Parents should make sure that their children understand how much they mean to them. The written word is a powerful way to express that parental love while giving godly guidance and direction.

42

CHILDREN BEWARE

"God doesn't seek for golden vessels, and does not ask for silver ones, but He must have clean ones."
Dwight L. Moody

As leaders, let's stop to consider just for a moment where we have been, where we are now, and what the future may hold for our country on this side of Heaven's glory. I would like to use this discussion as a "call to action" for Christians. What are some of the conditions and influences that have shaped the culture of American Christianity in the last five decades? The following questions may stimulate our thinking on this subject.

1. What impact has the breakup of the traditional American family had on our Christian heritage?
2. Has the welfare system created a crisis of reliance and servitude and had any direct or indirect part in obligating us to a master (government) that is not our own (God) while creating an overwhelming sense of entitlement?
3. What impact has removing prayer from public schools made on our Christian society?
4. What about abortion? Any impact here on the value of life?
5. What about our current public education system (government schools) where relativism and secular humanism are standard philosophies taught as the basis for human achievement?

6. What about those seemingly harmless thoughts about the American Dream and the impact that chasing wealth, prosperity, fame, and fortune has made on our society at large? How about the love of money and material things?
7. What about the accessibility of the internet, iPhones, iPads, TV 24/7, video games, print media, Hollywood, and cell phones? Do you think that any of this has helped to shape who we are as Americans?
8. Has America's cultural fiber and our spiritual center been cannibalized and replaced with the pleasures and distractions of this world?

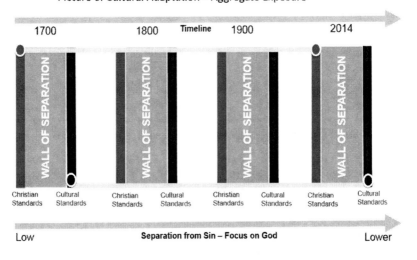

Let's say that we put two stakes in the ground during the 18th century (see illustration). The first stake would depict our cultural standards of the day: our morality, ethics, ways of thinking, music, role models, spirituality, what we do, what we say, and our love and concern for mankind. The second stake would depict the Christian standards for the exact same time frame. We would assume there would be a wall of separation between the Christian standards and the standards of the broader society in general.

Let us now fast forward to the 21st century and do the same comparison. Once again, we would assume there would be a wall of separation between the Christian standards and the standards of the broader society in general. We would argue that we would never embrace or remotely resemble the world.

Christian, don't you see that your stake has moved over time with society's stake? We picked up our 18th-century Christian stake along with our standards and decided to move them. We moved them to keep pace with society.

While I am not suggesting as Christians that we become some strange sub-culture with a cult-like notoriety, our standards have dramatically changed over the years at an alarming pace. I fully support living "in the world" and making an impact on people for Jesus Christ, but I oppose being "of the world" and looking like everyone else. Quite frankly, it is getting harder to distinguish between Christianity and everything else. Remember, God placed his heavenly stake in the ground at the beginning of time, and it has not moved an inch.

CHRISTIAN LEADERSHIP WORLDVIEW – PRINCIPLE #42

Leaders need to lead by example and not cave in to the pressures of life or to their peers. Stand tall in the face of adversity, and embrace what it means to be a Christian in the 21st century. It is the Christianity in God's Word. We are being bombarded by an aggregate exposure to the world's ways like at no other time in our history. This is a "call to action" to be separate from the world!

43

WHERE IS YOUR CHILD'S ANCHOR?

"The world has changed and it's going to keep changing, but God never changes; so we are safe when we cling to Him."
Charles R. Swindoll

We see the phenomenon of generational descent all around us. This has taken an unbearable toll on family relationships and values. The Christian heritage that once was taken for granted is now rapidly deteriorating across this great country. Conservative and godly parents are trying to reconcile where they went wrong. They ask themselves a countless number of questions:

- Were we poor examples?
- Did we live out our faith according to scripture?
- Should we have been more firm and demanding?
- Did we have them in church enough?
- How was our attitude?
- Did we show our children enough love?
- Were we in the Word of God daily?
- Did we show enough discipline?
- Was the walk of the Christian life evident to my children?

When parents see their offspring go the way of the world, it is a gut-wrenching experience shrouded in a covering of guilt and concern. Yet, they continue to love, pray, and give as much direction as possible to their loved ones. They want to yell and scream from the rooftops to save them from a lifetime of heartache and troubles.

So why are they pulling away? Many Christians speculate it starts with pride and the desire to be out from under the authority of parental guidance.

> "But we will certainly do whatsoever thing goeth forth out of our own mouth…" (Jeremiah 44:17)

> "In the mouth of the foolish is a rod of pride: but the lips of the wise shall preserve them." (Proverbs 14:3)

> "Only by pride cometh contention: but with the well advised is wisdom." (Proverbs 13:10)

> "Yea they are greedy dogs which can never have enough, and they are shepherds that cannot understand: they all look to their own way, every one for his gain, from his quarter. Come ye, say they, I will fetch wine, and we will fill ourselves with strong drink; and tomorrow shall be as this day, and much more abundant." (Isaiah 54:11, 12)

They want to go their own way, make their own decisions, and not feel like Mom and Dad are "ruling" their lives. Granted, while being able to make big decisions and wanting incremental autonomy are all part of the maturation process during the teenage years, where is the submission to authority in all of this? Pulling away from the things of the Lord is not the right answer. It is a path that leads to destruction. *Did I not teach them to be respectful and submissive to the Word of God?*

Parents do not expect their children to be just like them. However, they pray and hope that their children will be saved, develop core beliefs and standards from the Bible, have a concern for souls, and make spiritual contributions to the greater good of mankind. In short, they will make an impact for Christ in their individual spheres of influence.

Will there be consequences outside of an active and personal relationship with Jesus? Will my children be okay if they follow the ways of the world? The short answer is *no*; they will not be okay. There will be consequences for their actions. Sin is destructive. They will minimize their ability to impact positively the lives of other people for Christ.

> "But were mingled among the heathen, and learned their works." (Psalm 106:35)

> "Ye adulterers and adulteresses, know ye not that the friendship of the world is enmity with God? Whosoever therefore will be a friend of the world is the enemy of God." (James 4:4)

> "Thy way and thy doings have procured these things unto thee; this is thy wickedness, because it is bitter, because it reacheth unto thine heart." (Jeremiah 4:18)

> "I spake unto thee in thy prosperity; but thou saidst, I will not hear. This hath been thy manner from thy youth, that thou obeyedst not my voice." (Jeremiah 22:21)

Parents, do not give up hope. Continue to be the godly Christian examples that the Lord has called you to be. Do not compromise on any part of God's Word. Love and guide your children with Bible principles. When they reach into adulthood, continue to be frank with your children about godly standards and expectations. While you are not perfect, as parents, you always must set the tone and lead!

> "Let us search and try our ways, and turn again to the Lord. Let us lift up our heart with our hands unto God in the heavens." (Lamentations 3:40-41)

"But they that wait upon the Lord shall renew their strength; they shall mount up with wings as eagles; they shall run, and not be weary; and they shall walk, and not faint." (Isaiah 40:31)

Our Puritan forefathers had similar concerns for the second and third generation of Christians. Michael Wigglesworth summed up the impact of lukewarm worldly 17th century Christians in a popular poem of the day.³

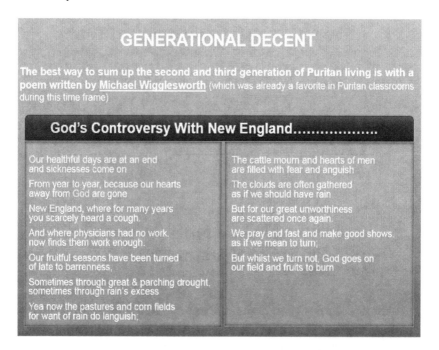

CHRISTIAN LEADERSHIP WORLDVIEW – PRINCIPLE #43

Christian parents need to set the example and the tone for their families until their dying days. We must encourage, give counsel, pray, and lead our families to higher ground. The future generations desperately need our guidance. Dare to leave a lasting spiritual legacy!

44

THE CONTENT FAMILY

"This is all the inheritance I give to my dear family. The religion of Christ will give them one which will make them rich indeed."
Patrick Henry

The Apostle Paul wrote, "Not that I speak in respect of want: for I have learned in whatsoever state I am, therewith to be content" (Philippians 4:11). This is one of the many great statements made by Paul through the Holy Spirit in his desire to serve the Lord faithfully. He acknowledged that, through experience and lessons of life, God had given to him everything he needed and had placed him in the exact circumstances for him to learn and become more like Christ. The Bible does not say that Paul was always content by nature. There was a learning process that Paul went through. That is why he said, "For I have *learned*…"

Are you learning to be content with your position in life? Are you content with the way the Lord provides financial security, food, clothing, and shelter for you? Or are you struggling to increase your social status and material gain because you have been lured into the world's philosophy of the "American Dream" where *more* is assumed to be better? I am not saying that to use your God-given abilities to provide for your families is wrong or even that having material possessions and wealth is wrong. However, there is a predominant tide in this world's system that encourages material competitiveness and material gain as the focus of life. *If I only had a bigger house, a nicer car, more income, and a lot more stuff, then I would elevate my position in life and be completely and totally satisfied and happy*, one thinks.

The world's system of today encourages competitiveness with one's neighbors. It is a philosophy that pushes people constantly to evaluate themselves against others, never learning to be content but always striving to have more and more. I once saw a worldly slogan that sums up man's desires here on earth: WHOEVER HAS THE MOST TOYS WHEN HE DIES, WINS.

I have posed this same question to myself many times before. *Am I content with the state that I am in?* I believe it is only when you come to this point in life of learning to be content that you can be a more effective servant for Him.

The Bible also says in the second part of Hebrews 13:5, "And be content with such things as ye have." We are a blessed people and a blessed nation that needs to set our affections "on things above and not on things on this earth" (Colossians 3:2).

CHRISTIAN LEADERSHIP WORLDVIEW – PRINCIPLE #44

We must be able to deflect the tug of the material world and be content with the things that God has blessed us with. Praise Him for His generous and abundant hand!

45

EXPRESSIONS OF LOVE

> *"O God, we praise Thee for keeping us till this day, and*
> *for the full assurance that Thou wilt never let us go."*
> *Charles Spurgeon*

His expressions of love are deliciously hidden
in the shadow of life's goings on.
Our joy is so full when we yield to His vision
and reside in Him all the day long.

He cares for us, He keeps us, and is constantly near
when we work, while we sleep, when we meditate, and while we pray.
His devotion has no limits, and He tells us, "Do not fear,
for I am the Master, the Creator of Heaven. Ye will stay."

We see His lovingkindness all 'round us, everywhere.
Our Lord is so magnificent. In awe should we be
of His presence, of His power, and of His gentle care
as He continues His longsuffering throughout eternity.

Praise the Lord. He really loves us with all His strength and might
because we are the chosen, the beginning, long ago.
His words of expression can be seen day and night.
The child of God is bound for heaven, for this we know 'tis so.

And as life's journey continues on, this gift of love of His,
we grow old, we grow wise, and begin to understand.
It's a holy responsibility, this expression of love to give.
For to exalt our precious Savior, it is His, this gift, God's plan.

CHRISTIAN LEADERSHIP WORLDVIEW – PRINCIPLE #45

This poem was written to remind Christians of a compassionate and loving God who never leaves us or forsakes us. He is constantly with us and desires that we seek His face. His love will be revealed to us in so many more ways in our day-to-day walk if we only would draw closer to Him. If only we will think about our God in every situation of life, we will find Him close by. We will find God in the small details of life along with those larger and more complex circumstances that seem too big to overcome. In short, God's love is always on display if only we would stop, look around, take it in, and give Him the praise! He has revealed Himself to us in His Word! Draw nearer still to him!

46

Babes in Christ Jesus

> *"Faith is deliberate confidence in the character of God whose ways you may not understand at the time."*
> **Oswald Chambers**

The minutes, the seconds, and days do they fly
as we look and take stock with questions of why.
Seems desperately fleeting, this existence on earth,
sin all around us, in spiritual dearth.

I plead, yet I cry for the end I am made.
Please show me, oh Lord, the paths You have paved.
You formed me and molded me in the image of You.
This duty I contemplate, a Christian brand new.

So I ask once again for more clarity at last.
Am I formed as a channel or some other task?
Have faith and belief that life's journey is set
to run this great race, a crown you will get.

With questions abounding, we say no to the flesh.
We ask, who are we? Is this but a test?
With all joy and sweet victory, we come to conclude
this life we are leading, in Christ to exude.

Exciting it is in that moment of time
when we realize life's mission; oh, life sublime.
It was there all along if only we asked.
Praise Him. Give Him glory. The future is cast.

CHRISTIAN LEADERSHIP WORLDVIEW – PRINCIPLE #46

This poem was written to depict the curious and inquiring minds of new believers in Christ. When we are first saved, there are so many questions to which we need answers. We strive to find that "perfect will" of God and the reason for our existence here on earth. While intellectually, we understand that we are new creatures in Christ, there is still a tremendous yearning for things unknown. During the early stages of the sanctification process, we begin to understand that we are called to a higher purpose, a purpose that many of us can't quite figure out. Yes, we want to serve the Lord, read our Bibles, pray, love others, and try to be more like Him. But the question of "what else" still remains. This poem simply acknowledges all of the questions of life for the new believer but concludes with a reminder of our duty to serve Him and glorify His Name.

Part 6

LEADERS ARE CONCERNED FOR
THEIR COUNTRYMEN

47

THE WHITEWASH IMPACT

"We all want progress, but if you're on the wrong road, progress means doing an about-turn and walking back to the right road; in that case, the man who turns back soonest is the most progressive."
C. S. Lewis

While recently journeying through the book of *Daniel* in the Old Testament, I was struck by how comprehensive and rich this book is when it comes to understanding peoples' motivations, ideologies, and passions. It's amazing what human beings are capable of doing to defend their belief systems and positions of authority. While individuals may be running in polar opposite directions with their beliefs, the veracity with which they cling to their perspectives can be unrelenting.

Spiritually speaking, our faith or the lack thereof helps guide and form our opinions and thought processes about how the world is ordered. When we get right down to it, either we believe God and the truth of His Word, or we don't. Each of us has a unique lens and worldview perspective that directs the way we think, make decisions, and ultimately the way we make sense of the world around us. I have found that most human beings are truly zealous, passionate, and protective when it comes to guarding their personal beliefs.

Oftentimes, that passion fuels our determination and motivates us to take dogmatic and unrelenting positions in which we are willing to take on and fight for our respective beliefs to the bitter end. As Christians, we should be prepared to defend and support the fundamentals of the faith at all costs. We should exude a dogged determination like no other and be ready to lay down our lives for the religious liberty that we have in Christ Jesus.

The Bible also teaches us that Jesus has given to us significant room to maneuver when it comes to personal convictions on issues that are not clearly evident in His Word.

In a nutshell, that is the wonderful love story we call Christianity. We embrace those who share a common belief and love for a risen Savior and the Word of God while celebrating the diversity so evident among the brethren. Yes, Christianity is considered a "big tent" religion with the opportunity for all to come to know Him as Savior. That is the way Christ designed it to be. Furthermore, we believe that there is great strength in diversity. While Christians are all sinners saved by the grace of God, we attempt to live out our faith with an ethical and moral center founded on biblical precepts.

> "Finally, brethren, whatsoever things are true, whatsoever things are honest, whatsoever things are just, whatsoever things are pure, whatsoever things are lovely, whatsoever things are of good report; if there be any virtue, and if there be any praise, think on these things." (Philippians 4:8)

Just think of the words in the above verse: honest, just, pure, lovely, good report, and virtue. What these words are describing is the playing field or the sandbox of the Christian life that we are given to navigate within. We are encouraged and commanded to do the right things based on the totality of biblical instruction. Praise God!

But what also has struck me from the book of *Daniel* is the motivation and will-power that unbelievers had in destroying the Word of God and all that it represented (past, present, and future). Satan clearly wanted to use unbelievers to obliterate the faith of God's people back then. The leaders of Daniel's day tried to destroy his authority, power, and godly influence in the kingdom. Entrapment, lies, jealousy, dishonesty, and political maneuvering were all part of the plot to take Daniel down.

What about today? Are we seeing this same approach played out through attempts to nullify and obliterate the authority and impact of God's Word? Is the world trying to whitewash our Christian faith? From a human perspective, doesn't it appear that we are playing on an uneven playing field?

Let's make sure that we do not miss a key part of the enemy's strategy in the book of *Daniel*. I will call it, "The Whitewash Impact." First, let me be clear about the strategy and tactics used by the enemy. They will do and say anything to further their agenda. Lying, cheating, stealing, and dishonesty are all in play. We saw it in Daniel's day, and we are seeing heightened evidences of the same strategic approaches in today's society. For example, in the first chapter of *Daniel* we find a verse that, on the surface seems relatively harmless:

> "Unto whom the prince of the eunuchs gave names:
> for he gave unto Daniel the name of Belteshazzar;
> and to Hananiah, of Shadrach; and to Mishael, of
> Meshach; and to Azariah, of Abednego."
> (Daniel 1:7)

Nothing too important; right? Those four young men who were potential leaders and among the brightest and best in Israel simply were given new Babylonian names by their conquering king. No harm, no foul; correct?

As a reminder, King Nebuchadnezzar of Babylon had just taken over and besieged Jerusalem. These four young men were now part of a conquered group of people.

But here is the reality of the situation: the actual conquering and takeover of Jerusalem was just the first step and a small part in a multi-phase whitewashing strategy to control the hearts, minds, and spirits of the people of Israel.

> Step 1: **Conquer** – Gain control and authority over
> the government and the land.

Step 2: **Pilfer** – Steal and redistribute their wealth and take captive the artifacts that make up the culture and what it stands for.

Step 3: **Speech** – Change the language of the nation of Israel where the tongue of the Chaldeans becomes the universal language.

Step 4: **Children** – Get to the children. Brainwash and whitewash the future leaders by changing the historical landscape and understanding (revisionists).

Step 5: **Names** – Change their names and what those names represented.

In other words, if you change the truth of history and repeat something over and over again for long enough, then reality begins to fade over time. We see this occurring today under the world's most repressive regimes. If you control the minds of the youth, then you can eventually control the entire culture's ideology and belief system. *Merriam-Webster's Dictionary* says that the simple definition of *whitewash* is "to prevent people from learning the truth about (something bad, such as a dishonest, immoral, or illegal act or situation); to gloss over or cover up (as vices or crimes); to exonerate by means of a perfunctory investigation or through biased presentation of data."

The one last significant detail that I would like to point out is related to the meaning of their individual names. Their new names were in quite a stark contrast with their original names. They went from having godly, Hebrew names to names that depicted Babylonian gods.

- Daniel means "God is my judge"; Belteshazzar means "Bel will protect"

- Hananiah means "God is gracious"; Shadrach means "inspiration of the sun"
- Mishael means "God is without equal"; Meshach means "belonging to Aku"
- Azariah means "the Lord is my helper"; Abednego means "servant of Nego"

CHRISTIAN LEADERSHIP WORLDVIEW – PRINCIPLE #47

So there is the spiritual war that we are waging, a war that goes well beyond the desire to compromise and get along with everyone in this present world. The minute we let down our guard, give in, and compromise any part of our faith, we are put at risk. We must not let today's whitewashing efforts go unchecked. We must stand tall and firm in the battle with our enemy, Satan. We do this by staying true to God's Word and not giving in. We must defend our rights vehemently as American citizens and the fact that this nation was founded as a Christian nation with Christian principles. Our silence suggests our apathy and an unwillingness to stand up for what we believe in. Our silence also allows the historical revisionists to rewrite and falsify American history. We are one nation under God! This nation needs Christ!

48

CASUAL TRENDS IN WORSHIP

"Refuse to be average. Let your heart soar as high as it will."
Aiden Wilson Tozer

As we are developing our *Christian leadership worldview*, we need to take to heart that the world is changing around us dramatically. The political, economic, social, technological, legal, environmental, and spiritual landscapes are shifting. While we understand that change is often a good thing, we need to be on high alert that we do not let our worship become casual in nature.

God wants all of us. First, He wants our hearts to be changed in the likeness of His image.

Second, He wants every fiber of who we are and the very essence of our beings to be in a state of complete and utter worship. Yes, every action, thought, deed, motivation, and especially our worship should be in 100 percent alignment with God's Word. He has given to us great liberty. We are no longer under the law but under the wonderful grace of God. However, with all of that liberty comes great responsibility.

I believe the verses below can help us begin to understand what the Lord expects from us when it comes to worship.

> "For brethren, ye have been called unto liberty; only use not liberty for an occasion to the flesh, but by love serve one another." (Galatians 5:13)

> "Who gave himself for us, that he might redeem us from all iniquity, and purify unto himself a peculiar people, zealous of good works." (Titus 2:14)

"This people draweth nigh unto me with their mouth, and honoureth me with their lips; but their heart is far from me." (Matthew 15:8)

So what are some of those key learnings from the above verses?

- We are called unto liberty.
- We are not to use liberty for fleshly desires.
- We are to love and serve one another.
- Christ redeemed us from all iniquity.
- Christ wants to purify unto himself a peculiar people, a people who are distinguished from the world.
- The Lord wants our hearts, not our vain and idle worship.
- The Lord wants our hearts, not a conformity to the things of this world.
- The Lord wants our hearts, not formalism.
- We are to be zealous of good works.

So with that as a backdrop, we can see how casual trends in worship along with a more ritualistic and formal approach to worship both could miss the mark of God's Word if the heart is not right.

So why all of the concern with a casual approach to worship? What are some of the implications from those casual trends we see sweeping across America?

- An effort to draw the masses with no concern for spiritual growth
- "Come as you are, and go as you were" with little evidence of spiritual growth
- P.C.-friendly churches
- "You're okay, I'm okay, and everything goes"

- In many instances, it appears to be nothing more than a social gospel.
- There is very little "meat" of the Word being preached as "meat" offends.
- Sermons have very little on the depravity of man.
- Living a disciplined, Christian life is not discussed.
- Nothing being preached about the Lord as our Judge
- It is predominantly a grace-only message.
- It has a seeker-friendly orientation.
- An overall lack of reverence for our Lord and Savior, Jesus Christ
- The Bible teaching and preaching does not melt and crush people like it used to because of cold and callous hearts.
- We see a club- and society-mentality rather than worshipping and glorifying God.
- We see lukewarm Christians with lukewarm standards.

CHRISTIAN LEADERSHIP WORLDVIEW – PRINCIPLE #48

The thing that most amazes me about the Bible is how balanced it is with the principles, promises, and precepts written. We learn that God is a God of love and of righteous judgment, and He is concerned with our hearts. He wants us to worship Him with our whole hearts. He wants all fleshly and selfish motivations removed. He wants us to be separate and distinguishable from the world by purifying us. A Christian leader must desire to stand tall in the face of adversity!

49

HAVE YOU NOTICED?

> *"The safest road to hell is the gradual one - the gentle slope, soft underfoot, without sudden turnings, without milestones, without signposts."*
> *C. S. Lewis*

Have you noticed just how clever and masterful Satan is as he passionately tries to deceive the world? Let there be no mistake; Satan has a clear agenda and plan to corrupt this world with his evil influences. In today's society, one of his most useful and subtle tools is that of "conditioning."

Have you noticed that decade after decade has slipped by, and we continue to tolerate much of his agenda? **Have you noticed** that we tolerate just enough for long enough until we become indifferent to the crafty ways of how he pushes his agenda? Whether it be through our television sets, music, dress, or a host of other life issues, we tolerate just enough until we become conditioned to the ways of Satan.

Have you noticed that Christians would argue vehemently against the ways of the world and its system but continue to "put up with" many of his tactics? Ask our older youth to think back several decades and describe the TV programming and movie standards of yesteryear. The world, notwithstanding Christians with good moral character, would not have tolerated the sin that we now so readily allow in our homes on a daily basis.

Have you noticed we have become conditioned and tolerant of the ways of this world?

> "Let no man say when he is tempted, I am tempted of God: for God cannot be tempted with evil, neither tempteth he any man." (James 1:13)

"But every man is tempted, when he is drawn away of his own lust, and enticed." (James 1:14)

CHRISTIAN LEADERSHIP WORLDVIEW – PRINCIPLE #49

My prayer is that each one of us would identify and be conscious of Satan's tactics and not let the world's standards become our own. This great conditioner is at work daily, so do not let him penetrate the hedge of God.

50
THE "ME" GENERATION

"Humility is not thinking less of yourself; it's thinking of yourself less."
C. S. Lewis

Since the Pilgrims first set foot on the shores of this new world, there has been a slow and steady decay in our submission to our Lord and Savior, Jesus Christ. Many would argue that the allure of the material world and the rugged spirit of individualism has crept in unawares to disrupt and tear down the cohesive fabric of society. Quite frankly, I think we have celebrated the "go-it-alone", self-made-man philosophy. Reaching out to others for help can only be a sign of weakness; right?

Clearly, our focus and desires have changed. No longer are we concerned about true collaboration, fellowship, and concern for our fellow man. The traditional has become anything but a raised eyebrow to what was once considered good, wholesome, and pure. Hard work and dedication have given way to slothfulness and entitlement.

Yet, while the selfishness and complacency lies all around us, we place our great hope in the power and impact of the gospel message, a message that lifts the soul and spirit to new and unforeseen heights. It is a message that provides a supernatural determination and discipline to move beyond the hopeless condition of "self" in order to exhibit a genuine love and care for the needs of others.

Only through the power of the Holy Spirit can we truly overcome the inclinations of our old natures. As leaders, let us renew our *Christian leadership worldview* perspectives!

Question: Has our Christian Leadership Worldview identity and focus changed over the years, decades, centuries?

OTHERS	➡ ME
Giving Glory to God	Self-Satisfaction
God Reliant	Self-Reliance
Giving & Supporting Others	Prosperity Seekers
Horizontal Covenant Relationships	Independence
Submitting Oneself............	Non-Conformists / Anti-establishment
Dying to Self	Pleasure Seekers
Absolute Truth	Relativism
Respectful	Disrespectful
Blessing to Others	Self-Gratification
Sense of community	Individualism
Wisdom/Skilled Living	Manipulation

CHRISTIAN LEADERSHIP WORLDVIEW – PRINCIPLE #50

Who is the most important person in this present world? Is it you?

51

THE CYCLE OF SIN

"The devil is a better theologian than any of us and is a devil still."
Aiden Wilson Tozer

I am so thankful that God in His Word goes to great lengths to remind us of the consequences of our sin. The Lord knows our human frailty and weaknesses. He knows that if we are not constantly reminded and challenged from His Word that we will fall back into similar patterns of sin. It is not only the sin that besets individual human beings, either. It is also the sin that destroys churches, communities, states, nations, and specific regions of the world. The Bible points out again and again that, outside of Christ Jesus, we will fall into that wicked cycle of sin that will end with righteous judgment. We will reap what we sow.

The leader's challenge is to be disciplined enough to stay in God's Word daily, be led by the Holy Spirit, and to develop such a God-consciousness that not a minute of the day goes by where His presence is not felt and noticed impacting our lives. When we do fail (and fail we will), we need to ask His forgiveness. We need to ask for His forgiveness so that we can be reconciled with Him. Leaders need to have such tender hearts that they are aware of their sin immediately.

> "If we confess our sins, he is faithful and just to forgive us our sins, and to cleanse us from all unrighteousness." (1 John 1:9)

"Thy way and thy doings have procured these things unto thee; this is thy wickedness, because it is bitter, because it reacheth unto thine heart."
(Jeremiah 4:18)

"Jerusalem hath grievously sinned; therefore she is removed: all that honored her despise her, because they have seen her nakedness: yea, she sigheth, and turneth backward." (Lamentations 1:8)

"Righteousness exalteth a nation: but sin is a reproach to any people." (Proverbs 14:34)

"If that nation, against whom I have pronounced, turn from their evil, I will repent of the evil that I thought to do unto them." (Jeremiah 18:8)

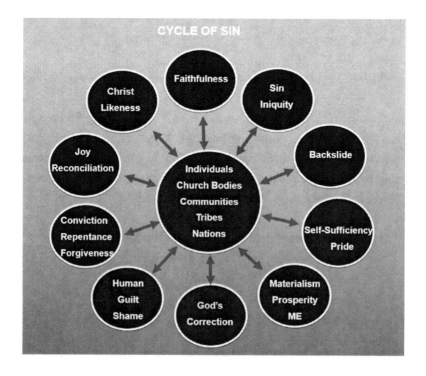

> **CHRISTIAN LEADERSHIP WORLDVIEW – PRINCIPLE #51**
>
> Make no mistake. The Lord will chastise and correct those that He loves and will remove His hand of grace where iniquity abounds. Why? He is a just God!

52

THE WORLD IS OUTRAGED! WHY?

"To be a Christian without prayer is no more possible than to be alive without breathing."
Martin Luther

The recent and continued public school slayings have sent a shockwave of fear through the school systems across the United States. Families in America are outraged and want to know the underlying reasons for the senseless massacre of innocent elementary and high school students. They fear for their children's safety.

If they earnestly contemplated the state of our society for a moment, they would see the deterioration of family values, the moral degradation prevalent in our society, and the freedom and so-called "rights" that are now being advocated for children at an early age. These problems help us to understand how these gut-wrenching atrocities could occur. The countless hours of "meditation" in front of video screens with ongoing violence, endless pounding of rock music that takes over the spirit, and the opportunity to witness tens of thousands of murders and other violent crimes without having to leave the comfort of our television sets can begin to scratch the surface of providing real explanations for these atrocities.

How did we come to this place in society and specifically in our public school system of today? For me, the answers to this question are very clear cut. Let us look at putting prayer back in our public schools as a starting point. Let's take the necessary steps to develop the spiritual foundation and spiritual center of our youth. Let us develop a *Christian leadership worldview* perspective and identity in our youth. Ever since prayer left our public schools, violence has escalated to an uncontrollable and concerning rate.

"Set your affections on things above, not on things on the earth." (Colossians 3:2)

"Pray without ceasing." (1 Thessalonians 5:17)

CHRISTIAN LEADERSHIP WORLDVIEW – PRINCIPLE #52

Prayer is good for the soul. Why would anyone not want to allow their children to have the opportunity to pray in a public school? Why would anyone not want their children to be able to experience spiritual growth? We are a Christian nation. We are one nation under God! Amen!

53

THE ADAMIC SIN NATURE OF MAN

"The Bible will keep you from sin, or sin will keep you from the Bible."
Dwight L. Moody

While the secular humanist philosophies abound with their grotesque depictions of a world where human reason, philosophical naturalism, and ethics must supersede all forms of religious order and faith, Christians can take comfort in the knowledge that Christ Jesus died on the cross for our sins. It is clear that the world (and Satan, who is the prince of this world) would have us believe that the good in man will overcome all obstacles and impediments to making this earth a better place to live. Through knowledge and a natural compassion for mankind, humans are expected to rise to the occasion to shower a humanist virtue of goodwill on all those around us. This is a belief that human morality is independent from a holy and righteous God.

The Bible teaches us a much different story. The Bible clearly emphasizes the wretched condition of man outside of a saving relationship with our Lord and Savior.

> "Wherefore, as by one man sin entered into the world, and death by sin; and so death passed upon all men, for that all have sinned." (Romans 5:12)

> "Knowing this, that our old man is crucified with him, that the body of sin might be destroyed, that henceforth we should not serve sin." (Romans 6:6)

> "For the wages of sin is death; but the gift of God is
> eternal life through Jesus Christ our Lord."
> (Romans 6:23)

While Adam's sin plunged the human race headlong into universal sin, we all participated in the fall of mankind. Positionally, we were actually sinning with him. However, it is through our obedience in Christ Jesus, by accepting that gift of salvation through the cross, that we too can be reconciled to Him and overcome eternal sin in our lives. One day, we will be with him in our glorified bodies.

> "Therefore being justified by faith, we have peace
> with God through our Lord Jesus Christ."
> (Romans 5:1)

If by chance you take a survey of your comparative human condition and muse that it could be worse, think long and hard about the natural condition of a man's heart. The Bible clearly tells us in Jeremiah 17:9 that "the heart is deceitful above all things, and desperately wicked: who can know it?"

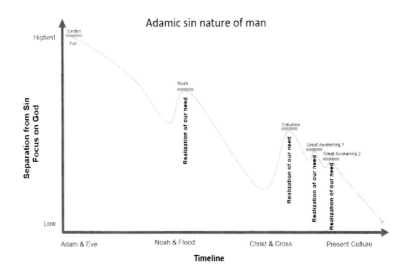

> **CHRISTIAN LEADERSHIP WORLDVIEW – PRINCIPLE #53**
>
> As a leader, you should continue to look in the mirror of His Word and allow the Holy Spirit to refine areas of need. While the Lord has allowed times in history of great spiritual introspection, until He comes, we will participate in a world of spiritual shortcomings.

54

AMERICA'S TIPPING POINT

"Truth will ultimately prevail where there is pains to bring it to light."
George Washington

At no other time since the founding of the United States of America have we had the level of opportunity we do now to change the course of history. This particular period in the development of our great country will set the stage of success for future generations. We are at the precipice of something unusual and extraordinary. Yes, America's tipping point is here and now.

Simply put, our nation is in the throes of trying to work out and determine what we want to stand for, what values and principles will be our guiding light and anchor, and what legacy we hope to leave for our children. The contrast of opinions on how best to move forward and achieve those results is varied and stark. Some argue that the fight is over political ideology, lifestyle choices, morality, ethics, or just common human decency. Others say that the battle is about individual preferences and the ability to do one's own thing. However, what this really boils down to is a fight for the spiritual center of our country. We are fighting for the souls of men and women. Everything else is merely an outcome (cause and effect) of our nation's lukewarm spiritual nature and lack of connectivity to our Savior, Jesus Christ.

The decisions we will make this year will have lasting consequences for decades and centuries to come. Positive spiritual change will occur only when Christian men and women decide to involve themselves in the process of America's renewal and spiritual rebirth. That rebirth will only take place when fundamental Christianity and absolute truth are the driving forces, the solid rock, and the foundation of our culture.

What I am suggesting is that we employ a traditional and "originalist" spiritual strategy in America that will help to preserve what this country has stood for through the years and the freedoms that we have enjoyed. Outside of that, it will be a long and slippery slope toward spiritual apathy, which ultimately will destroy our nation. If you think I am being an alarmist and melodramatic in my stated premise, please read on.

The words of Hosea in the Old Testament have never described more clearly the true state of a nation than they do the United States of America in the 21st century. The warning for our day should not go unnoticed or unheeded.

> "Hear the word of the Lord, ye children of Israel: for the Lord hath a controversy with the inhabitants of the land, because there is no truth, nor mercy, nor knowledge of God in the land, by swearing, and lying, and killing, and stealing, and committing adultery, they break out, and blood toucheth blood. Therefore shall the land mourn, and every one that dwelleth therein shall languish, with the beasts of the field, and with the fowls of heaven; yea, the fishes of the sea also shall be taken away."
> (Hosea 4:1-3)

> "My people are destroyed for lack of knowledge: because thou hast rejected knowledge, I will also reject thee, that thou shalt be no priest to me: seeing thou hast forgotten the law of thy God, I will also forget thy children." (Hosea 4:6)

Do you see the similarities compared to what is going on in today's world? There isn't much of a difference. However, I want to focus our attention on the last portion of this verse (Hosea 4:6) as it is a portion of Scripture that should give both Christians and non-Christians a pause for concern.

The foundation that we are laying as a nation will impact our children and grandchildren directly. Our offspring's spiritual destiny lies in the balance of our current decision making. The Bible is clear that, if we get so far off course from our spiritual center (God's Word and absolute truth), there will be dire consequences for future generations. God is telling us that, if we forget His law—which will lead to an overall lack of knowledge, spiritual depth, and true understanding—the end result will be apostasy and heretical living. When that occurs, God will remove His hand of grace from the United States of America. The result of getting further off course will be untold devastation and heartache.

Remember, God will never leave or forsake us. It is we who have left an Almighty God by our actions of disobedience.

America, what are we going to do? Will we continue with our selfish motivations, or will we change course and have a sincere desire to make our country spiritually relevant again, providing a thriving Christian bedrock for our children and the future state of our nation?

Christian, what are you going to do to make a real difference in our country? What choices will you make?

I believe that there are three primary courses of action (strategy) from which we can choose.

First, America can hold fast to a *Christian leadership worldview* and make God's Word the very center and existence of who we are as human beings. We can cling to the loving faith of Jesus Christ and be disciplined in our everyday living and walk with Him. We can go back to the traditional and "originalist" thinking of the godly men and women who had a hand in the creation of our great nation. This determination would be a God-honoring strategy to be sure.

Second, we can cozy-up to the standards of this present world, entirely forgetting that a Creator-God designed and spoke this universe into existence. This is a strategy that employs anti-God tactics and tries to confine Christianity to the four walls of a church building, a strategy that surely would please the prince of this earth, Satan.

A third approach, one that is so clearly evident in today's culture, is to try and do both at the same time. Live in the world, consciously enjoying all of its sinful pleasures, and then show up to a form of Sunday morning worship that nibbles around the edges. That way, church members don't have to be too committed to living a disciplined Christian lifestyle. They can have one foot in worldly living and one foot in Christianity (so-called) because it is all about them and their comfort! This, too, is a strategy that surely would please the prince of this earth, Satan—or, should I say, *does* please the prince of this earth.

The moral fiber and spiritual center of our country is being destroyed by this third choice. The fallout and results of this path (strategy) are obvious to anyone who is willing to be honest.

Let's consider a few of the prevalent societal issues that are decimating the core of the United States of America. Just think about the rampant nature of divorce, adultery, pornography, murder, theft, idolatry, and the extreme lawlessness that is pervasive in our country. For those who will not admit the obvious, that blind and selfish choice is clearly one of convenience, comfort, and personal satisfaction. Yes, this is the path that our country currently is following as a nation.

Fortunately, we have great hope and confidence in an active and living God who we trust and believe will intervene and change the course of human history. Remember, God uses man to accomplish His perfect will.

For true believers, the strategic choice to reconcile our country back to its spiritual center is obvious to us. We must get on our knees before the Lord and cry out to Him with fervor, immediacy, and sincerity… a cry that is so heartfelt that it shakes us to our core… a cry so loud and clear that the world stands up and takes notice. We must stand tall and let our light so shine before men. The following Bible verses challenge us to do exactly that!

> "Then they cry unto the Lord in their trouble, and he bringeth them out of their distresses. He maketh the storm a calm, so that the waves thereof are still.

> Then are they glad because they be quiet; so he bringeth them unto their desired haven. Oh that men would praise the Lord for his goodness, and for his wonderful works to the children of men!" (Psalm 107:28-31)

> "That ye may be blameless and harmless, the sons of God, without rebuke, in the midst of a crooked and perverse nation, among whom ye shine as lights in the world." (Philippians 2:15)

And yes, we need to be active in our pursuit of these God-honoring objectives to bring our country back to Christ. We need to follow the example of Jesus Christ Himself when He walked the face of this earth. Jesus came to this earth and upended and disrupted the conventional thinking of the day. Some would say that not only was He an activist in preaching salvation through Christ and Christ alone, but he was radical in His anti-establishment teaching and theology. He had a message and worldview that no one wanted to hear. He stood tall in the face of adversity.

Likewise, if God is going to use Christians as instruments to change the spiritual course of our country, we must be willing to take a stand. We, too, must be activists and anti-establishment in our approach to change. Our desire should be to bust up the establishment of this world's thinking and ideology to bring us back to a God-centered nation. The Founding Fathers understood that the backbone of our country rested in the faith that we have in a living God. They understood that our spiritual obedience would lead the hand of God to make and bless a great nation. They also understood that it would take grit, determination, and an uncompromising passion to fight for the things that made this country great in the first place. We are one nation under God. Life, liberty, and the pursuit of happiness are basic human rights that we must stand up and fight for. Will you stand in the gap and fight? Will you pull up your bootstraps and man-up?

> "And I sought for a man among them, that should make up the hedge, and stand in the gap before me in the land, that I should not destroy it: but I found none." (Ezekiel 22:30)

> "Watch ye, stand fast in the faith, quit you like men, be strong." (1 Corinthians 16:13)

Praise the Lord that the future of the United States of America looks bright! However, that shining light and beacon of hope will last only if we put our trust, faith, and hope in a risen Savior. America's tipping point is happening as we speak and unfolding before our very eyes. We are at a crossroads like at no other time in our nation's history. Let us unite as American citizens speaking with one voice to reestablish the spiritual center of our nation. Praise God!

CHRISTIAN LEADERSHIP WORLDVIEW – PRINCIPLE #54

Christian leaders must be engaged in the battle for the soul of America. Our contribution today in helping to shape the spiritual fiber of our country will help to lay the groundwork for a prosperous tomorrow.

Conclusion

It's Time to Step Up

For those who read this book in its entirety, congratulations! I hope that the issues and topics presented in this book have helped to provide a framework for leadership and successful living while challenging your thinking. Our consistent faith, prayers, and disciplined approach to life will take us to new spiritual heights never before realized. Sitting on the sidelines of life is not an option for true leaders. We must get involved and make a difference!

For those of you who have never before accepted Jesus Christ as your Savior, now is the time. Today is the day of your salvation! Ask Christ to save you and forgive you of your sins. Turn from your wretched sinful life and be a follower of Jesus Christ.

The Church that Christ talks about in the Bible has a big tent. There is room for all who trust Him as Lord and Savior. The Bible says that all have sinned and come short of the glory of God. Won't you trust Him today?

About Us

Christian Leadership Worldview International (clwi.org) offers high-quality leadership training and development solutions at affordable prices. Our desire is to help grow leaders around the world through one conversation at a time. We strive to impact organizations by improving employee morale, reducing turnover, increasing productivity, and fostering collaboration and teamwork as well as creating personal growth and self-improvement opportunities. In addition, CLWI takes a special interest in the development of young student leaders around the world.

Using a mission board, non-profit organizational model, CLWI has the flexibility to offer customized leadership solutions through a menu of options while being a low-cost industry provider. We are ready to serve the leadership needs of both employees and students alike. We are a Christian organization that uses Biblical principles and concepts as the foundation for organizational development and key learning experiences. Our focus is to point people to Jesus Christ, and we do it through training and development.

We believe that working through local churches is fundamental to who we are as an organization. As we help to grow Christian leaders on the one hand as well as evangelize and spread the gospel message on the other, we want to make sure that everyone is interacting with a local body of Christian believers as the Bible instructs us to do.

Our Logo

The prayer of Christian Leadership Worldview International (clwi.org) and its partners is that the logo represents a bold, compassionate, willing, and activist participant against a backdrop of global organizational need. CLWI wants our logo to signify the desperate need around the world for Christian leadership training and development in small-  to medium-sized organizations. We believe that many organizations of today are being left out of this needed spiritual growth opportunity as they focus primarily on financial, social, environmental, and technological concerns, leaving out the spiritual development of their people.

The silhouette behind the podium in the logo depicts the "call to action" for Christian leaders to stand up and get involved. While leadership does not always mean being front-and-center in a crowd, it does mean teaching, training, challenging, and motivating people to reach new heights of spiritual development. From those who lead through prayers kneeling at a bedside to those who are called to preach and teach the word in front of thousands, we must be willing to move beyond self for the benefit of others.

ENDNOTES

[1] Pew Research Center. http://www.pewforum.org/2015/05/12/americas-changing-religious-landscape/

[2] Quote by Ken Collier - http://www.goodreads.com/quotes/189164-just-two-choices-on-the-shelf-pleasing-god-or-pleasing

[3] Wigglesworth, Michael and Simolinski, Reiner, Editor, "God's Controversy with New England (1662, 1871)." Electronic Texts in American Studies. Paper 36. (Excerpts) http//digitalcommons.unl.edu/etas/36

CPSIA information can be obtained at www.ICGtesting.com
Printed in the USA
LVOW08*1955240516

489782LV00001B/2/P